A CLOSER LOOK

Learning More About Our Writers with Formative Assessment, K–6

Lynne R. Dorfman and Diane Dougherty
Foreword by Clare Landrigan and Tammy Mulligan

Stenhouse Publishers
Portland, Maine

Stenhouse Publishers
www.stenhouse.com

Library of Congress Cataloging-in-Publication Data
Names: Dorfman, Lynne R., 1952– author. | Dougherty, Diane, author.
Title: A closer look : learning more about our writers with formative
    assessment / Lynne R. Dorfman and Diane Dougherty.
Description: Portland, Maine : Stenhouse Publishers, [2017] | Includes
    bibliographical references.
Identifiers: LCCN 2017016466 (print) | LCCN 2017038616 (ebook) |
    ISBN 9781625311337 (pbk. : alk. paper)
Subjects: LCSH: English language—Composition and exercises—Study
    and teaching (Elementary) | English language—Composition and
    exercises—Study and teaching (Middle school) | English language—
    Composition and exercises—Evaluation. | Educational tests and
    measurements. | Educational evaluation.
Classification: LCC LB1576 (ebook) | LCC LB1576.D6348 2017 (print) |
    DDC 372.62/3–dc23
LC record available at https://lccn.loc.gov/2017016466

Cover design, interior design, and typesetting by Martha Drury

Manufactured in the United States of America

PRINTED ON 30% PCW
RECYCLED PAPER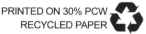

23 22 21 20 19 18 17   9 8 7 6 5 4 3 2 1

From Lynne:

For my mother, Betty, who helped me become a reader and writer by taking my sisters and me to the Free Library of Philadelphia on Wadsworth Avenue every Saturday morning through my junior high years for an armful of books. We shared books and read lots of poems. I was inspired!

From Diane:

Mrs. Krantz, my high school English teacher, taught me the power of reflection. She was never satisfied to simply attach a grade to my writing. Instead, she prodded me to think about what I did well and what I could do better next time. I owe her a debt I can never repay. This is for you, Mrs. Krantz.

CONTENTS

FOREWORD

As writing teachers, we want our students to live a "writerly life"—to see writing as a vehicle to appreciate the world around them, express their ideas, and share their voices with others. Formative assessment plays a crucial role in reaching this goal. When we know our students—their interests, their unique ideas, their strengths—we can help them flourish not only as writers but as confident young individuals.

A Closer Look shows us how to broaden the way we look at assessing writing in the classroom. This book helps us move beyond the numbers of a rubric and learn *how* we can assess so our students are fully engaged in the writing process. It shows how to take a step back and notice what is happening for our writers, the "why"s behind the behaviors they exhibit, their feelings about writing, and the craft moves they are using to try and bring more life and energy to their work.

One of the best parts of formative assessment is that it does not interrupt instruction; it's woven into the fabric of teaching and learning writing. From anchor charts and surveys to interviews and roving or peer conferences, the ideas in this book help us integrate formative assessment meaningfully into our daily routines.

In our book, *Assessment in Perspective: Focusing on the Reader Behind the Numbers*, we state that "questions further push us in the act of assessing." A focus on inquiry in assessment couldn't be more important. Diane and Lynne share ways to use inquiry to unite students and teachers in the assessment process. They write, "When a teacher lives in an assessment mode while teaching, a spirit of celebration and joy permeates the room. Children are clear about what they are learning, teacher feedback has shaped their work, and the learning becomes relevant. Best of all, our students see themselves as competent, accomplished learners." Diane and Lynne use this inquiry process to give students a new outlook—one that is supportive, thought provoking, and joyful.

As you read *A Closer Look*, you'll feel as if you are walking down school hallways and peeking into primary and elementary classrooms where kids are immersed in their writerly lives. Included throughout the book are videos, vignettes from other teachers about their experiences with formative assessment, and student work samples. These snapshots into classrooms provide a unique picture of how to assess in meaningful ways and help us gain new insights as teachers. In each example, we see the symbiotic relationship between assessment and instruction as one fuels the other to bring about purposeful learning for students. It's as if Diane and Lynne bring us in to sit alongside them and the teachers they work with as they assess and instruct.

We have long admired Lynne and Diane personally and professionally. They are generous mentors and lifelong learners with a passion for teaching writing. They are often the first to offer support and guidance to both new and experienced colleagues, and they are always on the lookout for ways teachers can collaborate to improve professionally. You will feel their encouragement, energy, and warmth as you read. You will find yourself thinking "That's so smart" or "I want to try that out!" Not only will they show you how to use formative assessment in your classroom, but they will make you feel like you can do it too.

Whether you are new to teaching writing, a seasoned teacher, or a coach, this book will show you how formative assessment improves instruction, honors student voice, creates a community of writers, and provides opportunities to authentically connect with students.

—Clare Landrigan and Tammy Mulligan

ACKNOWLEDGMENTS

Regie Routman tells us (2005, 239): "It is our job to insure that assessment practices lead to targeted teaching and improved writing." Regie's words help us explain why we wrote our book on formative assessment in writing workshop. We, too, believe that the purpose of formative assessment is to guide our instruction and experiences in ways that help our students grow as writers.

We warmly thank Dr. Mary Buckelew, our current director of the Pennsylvania Writing and Literature Project, for her encouragement. To our colleagues at the Pennsylvania Writing and Literature Project—Rose Cappelli, Brian Kelley, Tricia Ebarvia, Brenda Krupp, Teresa Moslak, Amy Hicks, Beth Stump, Rita Sorrentino, Frank Murphy, Katherine Lamothe, Diane Barrie, and Janice Ewing—we thank you for your snapshot into formative assessment and many words of wisdom.

So many educators wrote vignettes on formative assessment to add a chorus of voices to our book. Thanks to Mary Buckelew, Aileen Hower, Kelly Gallagher, Mark Overmeyer, Mike Bair, Shelly Keller, Gail Ryan, Kolleen Bell, Jill Dougherty, Joe Waters, Tammy Mulligan, Clare Landrigan, Stacey Shubitz, Susan Smith, Teresa Milrod, and Janet Wong.

Through our association with the Pennsylvania Writing and Literature Project, we became readers of professional books. These works continue to inform our instruction and give us the sense that we are never alone in the classroom while teaching writing and reading. We are grateful to so many authors who have informed our thinking, especially Don Graves, Don Murray, Regie Routman, Lucy Calkins, Carl Anderson, Nancie Atwell, Ralph Fletcher, Mark Overmeyer, Cris Tovani, Laura Robb, Tammy Mulligan, Clare Landrigan, Stacey Shubitz, Ruth Ayres, Barry Lane, Jeff Anderson, and Rose Cappelli.

Our work provided us with wonderful classroom snapshots.

From Diane: James P. Harris, Daniel Boone School District superintendent; Jenny Rexrode, principal of Daniel Boone Middle School; Dane Miller, principal of Amity Elementary School, and teachers Kris Endy, Amy Hicks, Teresa Moslak, Trish Ast, and Kathryn Lamothe. Thank you for your support and for your cooperation in allowing me into your classrooms. Working with your students was inspiring. Robert Milrod, Upper Moreland School District superintendent; Michael Bair, principal of Upper Moreland Intermediate School; Joseph Waters, past-principal of Upper Moreland Intermediate School, and teacher Kevin Black, thank you for your help and for making my visits welcome. It has been my pleasure to work with all of you!

From Lynne: Robert Milrod, Upper Moreland Township School District superintendent; Joseph Waters, past-principal of Upper Moreland Intermediate School; Michael Bair, assistant principal for the elementary schools; and Susan Smith, principal of the Upper Moreland Primary School, have been longtime supporters and friends. Thanks to the extraordinary contributions of kindergarten teachers Shelly Keller and Kolleen Bell, who help each student truly believe he is a writer. I learned so much from both of you. You modeled what it means to be a teacher of writers, sharing your writing every day. Thank you, Gail Speers, for many valuable conversations about writing in kindergarten. My heartfelt thanks to the remarkable second-grade teachers Kelly Gallagher and Dawn Costello and fifth-grade teacher Dan Monaghan, who provided fifth-grade peer conference partners for the second graders. Thanks to dear friend Sue Powidzki, for always pushing my thinking about teaching and writing and for her wonderful poster with revision reminders in the form of words and illustrations. A special thanks to Maribeth Batcho for allowing me to spend so much quality time in her second-grade classroom with her wonderful second graders and observe a master teacher in action.

A big thanks to Souderton Area School District Superintendent Frank Gallagher and to my valued friend and principal extraordinaire Gail Ryan who welcomed me with open arms. To my dear friend and colleague Brenda Krupp, a codirector of the Pennsylvania Writing and Literature Project, how can I thank you? Brenda, I learned so much from you and your students. It was truly a magical experience. I couldn't wait to arrive at Franconia Elementary School to be part of your writing workshop. I know you and Judy Jester will be writing a book together very soon. You have so much to share!

Thanks to our families.

From Diane: Thank you for your constant belief in me—my husband, Joe; children, Mark, Amy, Ed; and their spouses, Jill, Brian, and Amy. To my grandchildren—Collin, Maddie, Grace, Quinn, Conrad, Callum, Neil, and Alec—who make me smile just thinking about them. I am so grateful to you all for your love; I have the best cheerleaders.

From Lynne: Ralph, you make all things possible. Leigh and Gwen, I am very lucky to have you in my life. Diane and Willie, I know you love me and believe in me. That's very important to me. A big thanks to my family, including Merri and Rhonda, my Welsh Corgis. To my goddaughters, Alexandra Shinners and Brooke Shinners, and to my "other goddaughter" Caitlyn Shinners, and to their parents, Kevin and Jennifer Shinners—you are my extended family, and I love you always and forever. Thank you, Mary, Janice, Rita, Rosie, Linda, Tom, Nancy, Sue Po, Teresa Lombardi, Teresa Moslak, Reene Martin, Pat Smith, Karen Drew Rhoads, and Kate Lorenzi for your constant friendship and support. I had an entire team to support me!

Thank you, Diane, for being willing to give up so much time to write another book with me. I think we really collaborated to bring this book together in a format that will help teachers feel at ease with formative assessment and move their students forward as writers and learners.

To everyone at Stenhouse Publishers, thanks for your expertise, patience, attention to detail, artistic design, and sensible, meaningful advertising in your catalogs, conference displays, and magazines. Thank you Chandra Lowe, Nate Butler, Chuck Lerch, Jay Kilburn, Terry Thompson, Maureen Barbieri, Zsofi McMullin, and Grace Makley, our extended Stenhouse family. Of course, we want to extend our many thanks to Dan Tobin with wishes for continued success. Chris Downey, you were incredibly helpful and patient, always getting right back to our flurry of e-mails. Thank you to Martha Drury for designing and typesetting.

Bill Varner, you are absolutely amazing! We are so lucky to have you as our editor. Your gentle guidance, patience, and support do so much to help us move forward with these big projects. You are a dear friend and trusted colleague. Thank you, Bill, for everything you do for us. There simply are no words.

From Diane and Lynne: A special thanks to Ralph Abbott for his meticulous work filming and editing video clips included in this book.

INTRODUCTION

As teachers, we frequently spend time crafting "perfect" lesson plans. When we began our careers, sometimes we relied on those plans to carry the lesson. We may have noticed student writing behaviors, but we neglected to make note of them and to use our knowledge to inform our instruction. Formative assessment helps us recognize where our students are to help them realize where they need to go. It puts us all on track for taking ownership and responsibility for growing as learners (both teachers and students). In the process, students value learning and growth instead of just getting it done as quickly as possible and getting it right.

Today, new teachers have more responsibilities placed on them than ever before. Balancing curriculum demands while learning classroom management strategies is a daunting task. In *Visible Learning for Teachers: Maximizing Impact on Learning*, John Hattie (2012) cites the work of researchers Leahy et al. (2005) who asserted that the integration of formative assessment practices into across-the-day classroom activities of teachers will support substantial increases in student achievement. The purpose of this book is to provide formative assessment tools and strategies to use in writing workshop to help establish the "write" environment for a successful classroom where students are learning and growing. Teachers, both beginning and experienced, will become comfortable and skilled with formative assessment measures.

The act of writing lends itself to formative assessment. It is, indeed, a perfect fit. The writing process is recursive, not linear, and so we watch how our student writers navigate this process as they write across the types or as they produce multigenre writing. Teachers often lament that teaching writing is a difficult thing to do because the students enter our classrooms at different levels of sophistication, strategy knowledge, and writing fluency. The students in our classrooms learn at different rates and complete writing pieces accordingly. Formative assessment is the answer, allowing educators to respond to this reality by tweaking goals and instruction in order for students to grow individually. Writing workshop is a giant think tank of writers!

We invite you into kindergarten to sixth-grade writing classrooms as we work with students and teachers to provide ongoing feedback about content and process while focusing on specific areas of improvement, resulting in student engagement and reflection. Share our methods of collecting and managing information about student writers—their interests, processes, goals, strengths, and needs. Examine anchor charts used to document student thinking—collectively and individually—and teacher conversations about what these charts reveal about student learners' knowledge and recall concerning writing traits and writing types. Listen in as we confer with individual writers, small groups, and whole groups. Discover the power of peer and self-conferences. Learn when and how specific types of conferences are used to make a difference, not only in student products but also in strengthening relationships within the writing community. Our last chapter takes a look at quick, easy-to-manage formative assessment methods, such as admit slips and stop-and-jot notebooks that can be used in learning situations across the day, not just during writing workshop. Our thinking here is that assessment does not have to take a long time to be worthwhile.

SPOTLIGHT ON FORMATIVE ASSESSMENT

An Aha Moment: Formative Assessment, the Cornerstone of Learning

When I first began teaching in 1993, in what now feels like the Stone Ages (No Internet connection. Yikes!), I often overlooked the need for formative assessment. I mainly limited myself to anecdotal records and trained myself to carefully observe a few students each day to gain deeper insight into their learning and struggles. I believed this to be effective and prided myself on knowing my students and on being able to motivate them to want to learn. My students absolutely adored me, so I was quite sure that I was a terrific teacher and that my first year was off to a great start. In some ways, this was true. Motivating kids to want to learn is a big part of what we need to do as teachers. However, I saw the need to improve my instruction with writing. By the end of that year, I had decided to enroll in graduate courses in the teaching of writing through the Pennsylvania Writing and Literature Project. I started my second year of teaching third grade determined to get my students motivated to write.

I was a success at motivating my students to write. My kids begged to write each day. They loved the freedom to choose their topics and to write stories to their hearts' content. I was feeling rather proud of myself when I presented my reams of student writing at an inservice day to our curriculum director. He looked over my students' work and raised an important and rather obvious question: "What do you see as the greatest need with your students' writing?" Ah . . . Got me there. I only wanted them to write but had forgotten that I also needed to teach them *how* to write and how to do so effectively. I had clearly overlooked the fact that Kevin had written three consecutive stories about a "froggee" that liked to eat "flyes." The main words in each story were misspelled multiple times.

Because "invented spelling" was the catchphrase then, I had not been concerned; however, given that these words of significant importance had been used multiple times, it warranted a brief lesson. Although spelling is still not the first step in improving elementary writing, the aha moment for me was that I'd reached the middle of this school year and had not critically examined the deficits in my students' writing. Now, as a seasoned teacher of middle school eighth graders, I know that formative assessments are the cornerstone of lesson planning.

Amy Dougherty Hicks teaches eighth grade in the Daniel Boone School District in Southeast Pennsylvania. She is a National Writing Project Fellow and a Fellow of the Pennsylvania Writing and Literature Project in West Chester, Pennsylvania.

Indeed, we want to use formative assessment as a way to breathe life into our workshop, not to replace valuable instruction time with unnecessary assessment time. We do want to help our writers understand that they have ownership in the assessment process. Our students must also realize that they have responsibilities: setting and reaching goals, asking questions, sharing with others, revising their thinking, and taking risks to grow as writers and learners. That puts energy back into our writing time together.

As teachers, we want our students to be able to describe what effective writers do and how they improve over time. We want them to have a clear rationale for why writing is important and how it can help them now and later on as responsible citizens of our planet. Teachers, such as Jane Goodall, are patient observers and keen listeners who watch and write, watch and write. Just as Goodall recognized that all the chimps she studied were different, teachers understand that every student writer is different, and that student writers can greatly vary in attitude and in ability from one writing type to the next. Teachers gain the trust of their students by sharing their writing and conferring writer to writer rather than teacher to student.

As they gain that trust, teachers also begin to notice unexpected surprises about their student writers. Each day students do amazing things. They are growing and learning, and they know it. They know it because of the numerous opportunities for feedback from conferences, the anchor charts that make their learning public and permanent, admit slips, exit slips, self-evaluation pieces, surveys, and annotations students produce to get ready to respond to a text.

Formative assessment is an integral part of what we do across our day as seasoned "kid watchers" (Owocki and Goodman 2002). Three major goals of formative assessment in writing workshop follow:

- Monitoring student learning
- Using knowledge gleaned from observations, rubrics, checklists, writing samples to inform instruction (teacher)
- Using feedback to try new skills, to set goals, to evaluate progress toward goals, and to edit and revise writing pieces (student)

According to Peter Johnston, "The heart of formative assessment is finding the edge of students' learning and helping them to take up responsibilities for growth. Assessment isn't formative if it doesn't influence learning in a positive way" (2012, 49). According to Johnston, everyone in the learning community is responsible for providing the interactions that shape us as we grow. We believe these experiences, including each student's ability to assess his own learning and take note of the learning of his peers, will help all writers move forward. Noticing and appropriating successful practices in conferences, whole-group share, and reflection time is all part of formative assessment.

Formative assessment to track student progress is essential in twenty-first-century classrooms if we want to ensure writing successes for all students. As you read our book, examine the student samples and photos of myriad charts, surveys, and checklists. Think about the insights offered in the "Spotlight on Formative Assessment" vignettes we've included from classroom teachers, principals, K–12 curriculum and instruction directors, authors of professional books on the teaching of writing, and literacy consultants. We wanted you to hear many voices to help you think about this most important topic. Additional vignettes are available on the Stenhouse website. Use your QR code reader to access two-minute video clips on different kinds of conferences, including status of the class. We've also made the appendix and several of the figures throughout the book available as downloads at sten.pub/acloserlook. Enjoy your journey with us!

Chapter 1

THE RELATIONSHIP BETWEEN ASSESSMENT AND EVALUATION

> " When we think of assessment only as something that happens at the end of instruction, we miss many opportunities to become more effective teachers.
>
> —Mark Overmeyer, *What Student Writing Teaches Us* "

Assessment is an inquiry process. It requires time to gather information and to examine learning individually or collaboratively with colleagues, students, or both. Teachers and students can determine the progress toward short- and long-term goals to find ways to improve instruction, to set new goals, and to help to move learners closer to achieving success. As with any inquiry process, there is a place to begin and a place to end. However, in education, assessment is not the end. Finding an answer to one or several questions generates more questions. Therefore, assessment is the place where educators begin a journey to discover what their students know and are able to do. Assessment helps teachers determine what schemata (prior knowledge) already exist in their learners' heads, how they are achieving and growing in the present moment, and what direction or directions will be taken during a unit of study, a lesson, or a long-term project to make sure that all learners move forward. Quality assessment is an *ongoing* process of data collection that allows educators to make informed decisions before, during, and after instruction.

According to the *Merriam-Webster* online dictionary, *assessment* is the act of making a judgment about something. In education, the term *assessment* refers to the wide variety of methods that educators use to evaluate, to measure, and to document the academic readiness, learning progress, and skill acquisition of students from preschool through college and adulthood (*The Glossary of Education Reform*, www.edglossary.org/assessment). In *Leaders of Their Own Learning*,

Berger, Rugen, and Woodfin (2013) suggest that assessment should be a cooperative effort, not something done to students but, instead, something done with students. Assessment as a collaborative process gives students ownership in their own learning, establishing and strengthening relationships with their teacher and with their peers. According to Landrigan and Mulligan, "Assessment is more than a published test or tool that is administered formally. Assessment is also the data we collect authentically, every day" (2013, 2).

What is formative assessment? Although we have used the term *formative assessment* for more than five decades, educators cannot always agree on what it means. Carol Ann Tomlinson writes that formative assessment is "an ongoing exchange between a teacher and his or her students designed to help students grow as vigorously as possible and to help teachers contribute to that growth as fully as possible" (Tomlinson and Moon 2013, 11). Grant Wiggins makes the distinction about formative assessment with these words: "What makes any assessment in education *formative* is not merely that it precedes summative assessments, but that the performer has opportunities, if results are less than optimal, to reshape the performance to better achieve the goal. In summative assessment, the feedback comes too late; the performance is over" (2012, 5). The use of formative assessment by teachers and students is useful to make decisions about the direction and emphasis of ongoing learning. This kind of assessment helps teachers make instructional decisions throughout their day. It is immediate and has an impact on the learner, often giving him ownership in the assessment process. Formative assessment helps us know where our students have been, where they are right now, and where they are headed with our support and gentle nudges.

Leahy et al. (2005) talk about the effective strategies of formative assessment that teachers, students, and peers all do: clarify, share, and understand learning intentions and criteria for success. The teacher drives discussions, tasks, and activities that require students to meet some standard and accommodate new learning. Through effective and immediate feedback, the teacher helps the whole learner move forward.

Landrigan and Mulligan (2013) state that formative assessment helps both teachers and students to recognize what they know and what they don't know in a timely fashion. When that happens, students' needs can be addressed, and appropriate adjustments can be made to ensure success. We believe that peers and learners become resources for one another as they let in one another's thinking, noticing and appropriating problem-solving behaviors and creative thinking of their community members. In this way, students take ownership in the assessment process.

Formative assessment needs an environment in which students can become effective self-assessors of their own strategies and skills. This ongoing process of self-assessment will ensure that new understandings about their strengths, willingness to take risks, and skill areas that deserve close scrutiny will emerge along the way. Such reflection leads to a development of a growth mind-set in our writers. They need to see that they are always growing: taking risks, working hard, staying with a task until it is completed, and reflecting. The most energized writing workshops depend on young writers who take responsibility for and ownership of their growth (Mraz and Hertz 2015). Students need to keep an open mind to critical feedback, make an effort to remove biases ("I never was any good at writing."), listen attentively to their writing community, and be willing to try new things. The writing workshop format lends itself to a growth mind-set persona because writing takes place over time, feedback is continually offered, student writers are teachers of writers in peer conferences, and opportunities for reflection are built in to the daily routines. We are all fundamentally a mix of fixed and growth mind-sets, and we benefit from acknowledging the mix in ourselves and in our students.

Writing workshop offers many opportunities to engage in formative assessment practices. Interest surveys and inventories, teacher and peer conferences, and "clipboard cruising" observations (roving conferences or anecdotal note taking), self-evaluations, and student work, including multiple drafts, planning sheets, and writer's notebooks are all frequent, ongoing formative assessment. "Formative assessment is a constantly occurring process, a verb, a series of events in action, not a single tool or a static noun" (NCTE Position Statement 2013, 3).

When students are writing their drafts, they need feedback appropriate to that stage of their writing. For example, if Caitlyn is writing about her family's trip to Disney World and she begins with the trip to the airport, conferring with Caitlyn about her topic and the point she wants to make to her readers is the appropriate strategy at that time. If, during conferring, the teacher notices that a number of students seem to have Caitlyn's difficulty in narrowing the topic and making a point, that knowledge informs instruction. Assessing the needs of our students, in this case the need to narrow a topic for greater specificity and clearer message, may drive the grouping of future mini-lessons. In other words, not every student in the class will need more instruction about a tighter focus.

Formative assessment provides opportunities for teachers and students to imagine, create, inquire, collaborate, explore, question their thinking, and challenge themselves. For example, suppose Neil writes what he thinks is an informational piece on the rain forest after a unit of study. The teacher will use this piece to assess learning and to assign a grade to each child for this science unit and for writing. The information is complete, accurate, and illustrative. Nevertheless, the teacher notices that the writing is a multigenre piece. Its global structure is narrative, embedding characters that journey to the Amazon rain forest to study plants and animals. The teacher can assess the abundant knowledge, powerful voice, variety of sentence patterns, engaging content, and sharp focus around this writer's point. However, when it's time to evaluate Neil and give him a grade, what should this teacher do? The type of writing is clearly narrative with fictional characters, a problem, and a conflict. Yet, Neil masterfully embeds necessary information as description, anecdotes, statistics, and quotes from experts into his writing. Perhaps, the teacher sees an opportunity to demonstrate narrative writing as one way to impart information. She can use *Sky Boys: How They Built the Empire State Building* by Deborah Hopkinson (2012) to show how information can be framed with a story opening and close, in accordance with the Common Core Anchor Standard 5, which states: "Develop and strengthen writing as needed by planning, revising, editing, rewriting, or trying a new approach." Could this piece of writing be viewed as a new approach to informational writing? Together, with the students, the teacher can create an anchor chart about Neil's piece and *Sky Boys* to study new approaches to informational writing. The next day the teacher can refer to a chart already created regarding characteristics of informational writing to allow students time to reflect and compare points that are the same and those that are different. Clearly, this classroom conversation, as a result of Neil's piece, shows how assessment can inform instruction, often benefiting the larger writing community, not only one individual learner.

As Duckor reminds us, teachers need to become familiar with student learning progressions. In other words, "how students work themselves through the building blocks of a big idea" (2014, 32). When we listen to our students as they solve their writing problems, we may not only discover their learning steps but also uncover strategies for moving other writers forward.

Formative assessment can become a tool for setting new goals. Caitlyn is writing about her family's trip to Disney World. The teacher notices that now she has mastered the art of narrowing down the topic and is able to make a point. It does not read like a litany of "And then I . . ." paragraphs. The teacher praises her for having mastered an important goal and notes it in her conference notebook. The teacher observes that Caitlyn begins most of her sentences with subject noun followed by the verb. During this conference, Caitlyn and her teacher discuss the idea of setting a goal to revise for sentence variety. As the teacher has noticed this same difficulty in other fifth graders, her assessment leads her to create several mini-lessons about starting sentences in different ways: beginning with prepositional phrases, using –*ly* adverbs, and beginning with dependent clauses (see Dorfman and Dougherty 2014).

The examples of Neil's and Caitlyn's writing enable their teachers to make good decisions about what the students needed to do next to move forward as writers. The support from their teachers enabled them to take risks and to try something different. They believed they could succeed. Each revision became more purposeful. As Neil and Caitlyn reflected on their revisions, they felt better about themselves as writers and grew in confidence. When a community exists that honors approximations and views them as windows to learning opportunities, writers are free to experiment, to collaborate, and to try new approaches. This does not mean that students should not be in the habit of self-editing. For instance, students can self-correct for punctuation, capitalization, and spelling because that's what writers do. They always reimagine the possibilities. Writers are decision makers and need to make choices that work for the piece they are writing. Use of mini-lesson notes and writer's notebook observations concerning craft moves, grammar, and mechanics should be encouraged and expected. Teachers should encourage independent editing as a writerly habit.

SPOTLIGHT ON FORMATIVE ASSESSMENT

Formative Assessment Solidifies Learning

As an elementary principal, I know it when I see it—immediately. When walking into a classroom I can instantly detect if children are doing work that matters and if they have a strong sense of how to improve their work. Implicit in this picture is a teacher whose instruction and feedback are anchored in ongoing formative assessment.

And here is what I see:

- A room that "hums" with engaged, happy learners who have voice and choice in the work they do
- A teacher who is with the children, conferring and offering immediate feedback to them as readers and writers
- A teacher who listens to the students, observing them during turn-and-talk partnerships to see who understands and who needs more scaffolding
- Children who actively assess themselves, using rubrics to compare their answers to the sample answers on the rubric
- Children talking together, offering constructive feedback and praise for one another's work
- A teacher who notices—what children say, what they write, what they are doing—to craft the next instructional steps

In a recent classroom observation, a second-grade teacher was showing children how to insert line breaks into their poems. After the mini-lesson, complete with guided practice, the teacher circulated around the room, taking notes, and checking work to see who "got" what she taught. This teacher masterfully offered clear, specific feedback to each child as she went. Noting who was having difficulty, she pulled a small group to the rug, retaught the lesson with manipulatives, and had them try again. All of a sudden a high five and "Awesome!" signified that one little guy finally understood. This is formative assessment, and it solidifies learning.

When a teacher lives in an assessment mode while teaching, a spirit of celebration and joy permeates the room. Children are clear about what they are learning, teacher feedback has shaped their work, and the learning becomes relevant. Best of all, our students see themselves as competent, accomplished learners.

Gail Ryan is past-principal of Franconia Elementary School of Souderton Area School District in Montgomery County, Pennsylvania.

Of course, for teachers, perhaps the most important routine leading to students' learning from their drafts is providing timely feedback. According to Wiggins (2012), the most effective feedback is timely, ongoing, specific, addressable, and content rich. Of course, we agree! It does little good to suggest to Caitlyn that she needs to narrow her focus and make a distinct point after the paper is returned with a final grade on it. That feedback is too late to motivate the student to engage with the piece of writing again. Unfortunately, the final grade is often a dead end for a student, and if the student receives a grade he doesn't understand because the feedback lacks specificity, the paper hits the circular file almost immediately. Writing teachers who write view multiple drafts as opportunities to provide focused feedback. They free their students to take risks to try out new strategies, scaffolds, and directions with their writing. Quate and McDermott (2014, 63) state that effective teachers view failure as a productive stepping-stone to success.

Evaluation, or summative assessment, comes further down the road, and often takes the form of a final grade. Effective evaluation is an ongoing process that compares one student's performance to all the other students in the class. It occurs at one moment in time and involves both qualitative and quantitative measures. Rubrics, checklists, and sometimes collaborative criteria form the basis for this grade. In education, evaluation should include written comments, suggestions, or points that help students understand their final grades. The final evaluation looks at the overall quality of a piece of writing and the skills and strategies the student has applied to his writing. Even though no piece of writing is ever done and only driven by deadlines, evaluation provides closure to the writer and allows him to move on to another piece of writing. It can be used, like formative assessment, to drive instruction if it is not viewed by the teacher or students as once and done. In other words, the piece of writing is not as important as what the students can learn from it and take with them to future writing pieces. In most instances, feedback teaches the writer. The individual writing task engages the student to achieve a challenge or a goal.

Standardized writing tests are summative assessments that measure a student's writing ability and provide some valuable information about a student's skill level as compared to other students in his grade level across our country. At the end of a unit of study, summative assessments are used to evaluate which students reached the learning targets and which students did not. They cannot do much to customize instruction to help each student grow as a writer each day and each year. That is the job of formative assessment.

The following chart from NCTE's Position Statement on formative assessment may serve to clarify our thinking about what authentic formative assessment in writing workshop *is* and *is not* (2013, 6). The thinking behind these descriptors will help teachers, language arts supervisors, and curriculum mapping committees insert new assessments that support a deeper understanding of what students do and what they need to learn how to do to be successful:

Formative Assessments *Do*	Formative Assessments *Do Not*
Highlight the needs of each student	View all students as being, or needing to be, at the same place in their learning
Provide immediately useful feedback to students and teachers	Provide feedback weeks or months after the assessment
Occur as a planned and intentional part of the learning in a classroom	Always occur at each time for each student
Focus on progress or growth	Focus solely on a number, score, or level
Support goal setting within the classroom curriculum	Occur outside of authentic learning experiences
Answer questions the teacher has about students' learning	Have parameters that limit teacher involvement
Reflect the goals and intentions of the teachers *and* the students	Look like mini-versions of predetermined summative assessments
Rely on teacher expertise and interpretation	Rely on outsiders to score and analyze results
Occur in the context of classroom life	Interrupt or intrude on classroom life
Focus on responsibility and care	Focus on accountability
Inform immediate next steps	Focus on external mandates
Allow teachers and students to better understand the learning process in general and the learning process for these students in particular	Exclude teachers and students from assessing through the whole learning process
Encourage students to assume greater responsibility for monitoring and supporting their own learning	Exclude students from the assessment process
Consider multiple kinds of information, based in a variety of tools or strategies	Focus on a single piece of information

Teachers who use formative assessment in writing workshop and across the day wherein writing is used to record thoughts, observations, and opinions understand the time required to write, to reflect, and to give effective regular feedback. They understand that the writing process is not strictly linear but recursive: at any point, a writer could go back or move forward. Writing activities do not always have to culminate in finished products to be useful. A lot of writing is informal—its purpose is reflective thinking. Teachers can trace the journey of a student's thought processes to discover more about how a student thinks and integrates information.

Why is it so important for teachers to be familiar with the writing process? There will be a great deal of variability in students' confidence and writer self-esteem, cognitive abilities and grammar knowledge, styles and approaches. Familiarity with process affects teacher expectations and their teaching in four important ways:

1. Process-oriented teachers know students need regular and frequent practice in a variety of writing types (modes).
2. These teachers emphasize the writing process, especially prewriting and revising in their assignments and instruction, providing time for conferences along the way.
3. The more teachers know about process, the more they understand that writing is hard work. What we want for students (and for ourselves) is to understand their own writing as a process of choice.
4. Along the way students will make decisions. Writing is thinking, and the more we know about how our students think and how they make choices, the better we are equipped to adjust instructional practices to suit their needs and wants.

In a writing workshop classroom, almost all assessment will be formative. Our job as writing teachers is to help students become the best writers they can be, not merely to achieve grades. In classrooms driven by formative assessment measures, students learn to become more reflective about their writing practices. They see possibilities and are willing to consult with peers and explore possibilities on their own. Teachers can monitor and adjust daily. The result is improved student achievement.

Chapter 2

SURVEYS, INVENTORIES, AND LETTERS

" Helping students develop attitudes and skills necessary for autonomy as learners is [also] beneficial because it leads teachers to be more metacognitive about the teaching-learning process. "
—Carol Ann Tomlinson and Tonya R. Moon,
Assessment and Student Success in a Differentiated Classroom

What are the important, long-lasting effects of formative assessments in writing workshop? Do they help student writers understand that writing is a valuable tool they will use throughout their lives? Do they understand that writing is a means to achieve goals and develop an understanding of themselves and others? Interest surveys and inventories help students develop a writer's identity, to consciously declare, "I am a writer." Surveys, autobiographical sketches, and time lines can help the student and teacher discover more about attitudes, interests, motivation, and self-concept, which all contribute to students' successes or failures.

Writing Inventories: A Useful Tool

Writing teachers have the opportunity every day to learn something new about their students. Within the writing community, teachers demonstrate writerly behavior, they engage in writerly talk, and they observe their students as they write, talk, and share their work. Early in the year we invite students to share with us what they think and know about writing. A writing inventory allows teachers to assess their students' prior knowledge and recall writing formats and skills. An inventory enables the teacher to learn more about students' attitudes toward writing narratives, opinions, and informational pieces.

The writing inventory can be used more than once during the school year, and its purpose is twofold. For teachers, the inventory is a way to discover information about how students feel about writing and how they feel about themselves as writers. This knowledge is important because it will help teachers create specific writing opportunities to motivate students and provide access to information that will help teachers understand prior experiences. For students, the inventory enables them to reflect on what they already know about writing and how they feel about the writing process. Responses to these inventories should be shared in the classroom because sharing provides the vehicle for discussing the anxieties, fears, and stumbling blocks students face when they write. Sharing frees students to be honest. They find out they are not alone—that others have these same feelings. The teacher should complete the inventory as well to be a part of this community sharing.

Finding Out What Our Students Think Writers Do

Regie Routman (2000) teaches us that student writers need to be reflective when they make decisions about their own writing, as well as the writing of their classmates.

In Shelly Keller's classroom, kindergarten students were asked one question in order to gather information concerning their thinking about writing and what writers do. In primary grades, a writing inventory can consist of one or two questions. For our younger students, the physical act of writing—forming letters, leaving spaces between words, thinking about where to put end punctuation, and deciding on when to capitalize a letter—is a big chore. Younger students do better with less. Shelly conducted this inventory as part of a one-on-one conference in late fall and recorded her students' responses. She asked her students to complete this thought: A *writer* . . . To get them started, Shelly suggested, "Think about our writing workshop. What are the kinds of things you do as a writer during workshop time?"

Consider the kinds of background information Aliana possesses as a kindergartener. Many items on Aliana's list had been discussed during a unit on informational writing. Some of the items are small mini-lessons that Shelly, and in all likelihood, Aliana's nursery and prekindergarten teachers, may have discussed and demonstrated, such as the value of reading your writing aloud and how a writer prepares to write. Shelly and Lynne were sure they knew why Aliana used the word *idea* in several places. The day before Aliana's conference, Shelly had shared *What Do You Do with an Idea?* by Kobi Yamada (2013). Clearly, Aliana was thinking about this text when she talked with Shelly.

A writer...
1. thinks about her idea.
2. plays with her idea.
3. draws pictures.
4. talks about her idea.
5. blends sounds.
6. practices writing.
7. reads her piece out loud.
8. shares her idea with everybody.

You can also see that Aliana has some understanding of a writing process. She knows that writers plan their piece and do a good bit of thinking. She also understands that writers need words. Words are important. Aliana grasps that writing is not an isolated activity—something to do alone. Writing ideas are discussed with trusted others. Consider Liam's list and the kinds of things he feels are important:

A writer...
1. needs to know lots of words.
2. needs three pages.
3. needs a starting place.
4. needs a middle and an end.

Liam has certain perceptions that may become a future mini-lesson. For example, there really is no correct number of pages just as there is not a magic number for the number of sentences in a paragraph. Sometimes, teachers will throw out a number to give students a guideline. Even college students continue to ask, "How many pages do you want?" Often, we may address issues of writing fluency in primary grades, so one of our observations may be about the length of writing pieces. Encouraging fluency before form and correctness is not a new idea. For a student who is having difficulty with fluency, placing an X on a line on the paper and asking the student to write to that mark will give him an achievable goal. The next time, move the X so the student needs to write a little more. Attaining a degree of comfort with placing words on a page is important. Sometimes, it is necessary to give students an opportunity to write at a computer or on an iPad. Other times, it is a good idea to be able to record students' words for them or let them talk their story into a recording device.

In January, Shelly conducted another inventory. Her kindergarteners surprisingly were quite interested in putting down their thoughts about what writers do and wanted to share them aloud in whole group. They had many strong points that demonstrated their working recall of writing knowledge.

From Olivia: *A wrtr wrt in a ntbk and sw wat you fel and thnc.* [*A writer writes in a notebook and shows what you feel and think.*]

From Liam: *Gd wrtrs red ther writeing and write a gan!* [*Good writers read their writing and write again!*]

From Keagan: *Read ofr yur wrting. Look at yur wrting because you mut mak a mustak.* [*Read over your writing. Look at your writing because you might make a mistake.*]

From Giovanna: *A wrtr sud yos a plan.* [*A writer should use a plan.*]

From Zaire: *A wrtr wrt al the tim.* [*A writer writes all the time.*]

From Nicholas: *A [writer] neds to read lots uv books. A wrtier neds to read all the time. A good wrtier neds to read evrything!*

When Lynne asked Nicholas to explain his comment about reading all the time, Nicholas said, "You need to use your imagination. I like to write different kinds of things—sometimes information, sometimes stories. Sometimes I make things up, and sometimes they are true. I am making a book about a turtle that is looking for red rocks. I write what I want to. You just need to write about things you know about. I know a lot of things because I like to look at books, even if I can't read them."

The next day, Lynne asked students to share their thinking with the whole class. Students talked about the kinds of things that held them back or made them afraid when it was time to write. The two main concerns, stated in many different ways, were not knowing how to spell the words and not being able to come up with an idea to write about—feeling stuck—and looking around the classroom to see other students writing while your page is empty.

Shelly and Lynne noted that revisiting a focused lesson or several focused lessons on how to find topics to write about, as well as a mini-lessons on spelling strategies, might be in order. Shelly wanted to revisit the chart posted in the front of the room where student writers demonstrated their bravery to spell difficult words without asking for help (see Figure 2.1). Over the course of the next several months, Shelly continued to post a new chart. As she conferred with the kindergarten writers, she noticed those writers who tried to spell difficult words without asking for help. These students placed their words using invented spelling in one column. Before the end of writing workshop, Shelly wrote the adult spelling in the next column. Whenever a chart was filled, Shelly asked her students to applaud the writers listed on the chart for their spelling bravery. This would occur at the end of writing workshop as they gathered to share on the rug. Most of the cheers were silent, like a very quiet round of applause (students moved their hands in a circle while quietly clapping) as Shelly read the names of each student and the word he tried to spell. Often, students used this list for editing purposes, an additional benefit.

In Brenda Krupp's third-grade classroom in early spring, students met as a community of writers to respond to the question: *What do writers do?* Brenda asked them to take a few minutes to write in their notebooks and then to take

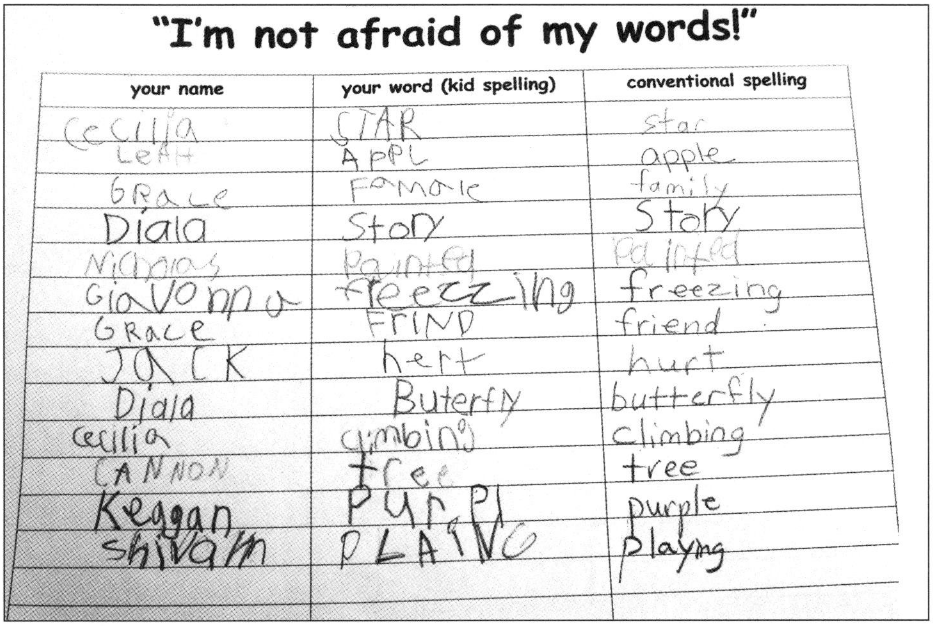

Figure 2.1
Spelling Chart in Shelly Keller's
Kindergarten Class

"I'm not afraid of my words!"

your name	your word (kid spelling)	conventional spelling
Cecilia	STAR	star
Leah	APPL	apple
GRace	Famole	family
Diala	Story	Story
Nicholas	Painted	Painted
Giavonna	freezzing	freezing
GRace	FrIND	friend
JACK	hert	hurt
Diala	Buterfly	butterfly
cecilia	cimbing	climbing
CANNON	tree	tree
Keggan	Purpl	purple
shivam	PLAINC	playing

a few minutes to turn and talk. Brenda could see what they valued as writers after surveying the whole-group responses she had charted:

Writers . . .

- build writing muscles by writing every day.
- find seeds of ideas everywhere. (When Brenda asked for examples, her students named places, including airports, markets, malls, playgrounds, parks, restaurants, school cafeteria, and soccer field.)
- carry a notebook everywhere.
- are alone to write and think.
- spend time revising.
- spend time planning.
- are part of a writers' group.
- reread their favorite books.
- look at a mentor text for a craft move.
- get it down and think about editing later.
- want other people to read what they wrote.

Just before Brenda called for responses, Lynne had listened in to this conversation:

Jax: I use my notebook to try things out.

Dan: I do, too. When I keep writing, I think of more things.

Bryce: Sometimes, I draw first and write second.

Clare: Writers make lists or neighborhood maps or sketches to find topics to write about. They find seeds everywhere!

Bryce: Writers never give up.

Jax: I never give up. I just try something new if the first way doesn't work.

Dan: I try different things, too. Sometimes, I don't finish a piece if I don't like it.

Writerly conversations like this can tell us much about our students' confidence levels, their priorities, and their misconceptions and inform us about their knowledge about writing process. These conversations help us find partners for peer conferring. They help us set goals for our students. These conversations always help students to establish and maintain a writing identity, as well as develop a growth mind-set.

Autobiographical Sketches

In addition to surveys, autobiographical sketches are another way to understand students' writing background. Ask students to write about themselves, discussing successes and failures in a comfortable format that could include a friendly letter, a narrative, a top-ten list, or a poem. Students can also create a time line on which successes are posted above the line and failures are posted below the line. Students can start anywhere—as early as nursery school or as late as the last grade they completed—whatever they are comfortable sharing with you. In this way, teachers have a starting point to begin to think of ways to engage their student writers in the act of writing. After all, we want engaged students, not compliant ones. The difference between engagement and compliance is as wide and as deep as the Pacific Ocean.

Consider this piece of writing by Selena, a fifth grader, in her writer's notebook and what we can learn from it:

> I really do like to write, but most of the time I enjoy writing poems and stories. It's important to have the perfect notebook–just the right size and with big spirals so when it opens, it is flat on my desk. I like to find journals that are smooth, shiny, and covered with flowers or maybe all pink or all purple. I have filled many notebooks and I save them all in a big wooden chest in my bedroom. I may write books one day, and Dr. Dorfman once told us that most story writers are writing about things that happened to them during their childhood. So I think it's a smart idea to start saving those notebooks now. Writing is my favorite subject. I am a good speller and I have great ideas. I think I could write all day and never get tired of writing!

From this sketch, we discover that Selena likes to write stories and uses her personal childhood experiences as the basis for her stories. She saves her writer's notebooks in a trunk, which may mean that she likes to reread what she wrote and that she possibly writes beyond the school day. This idea could be explored in a conference. She describes the kinds of notebooks she likes to write in. This information helps teachers understand that notebooks, whenever possible, should be chosen by the writer. Selena doesn't mention writing anything besides narratives, so a conversation could follow about what other things she might like to try this year. Clearly, a great deal can be learned from an autobiographical sketch.

Interest Surveys Help Us Differentiate Instruction

In the beginning of the school year or semester, gather information about student interests, especially to help struggling or reluctant writers to find topics to write about. One easy tool is a four-square interest survey that can be created on different sizes of paper, depending on the grade level. Younger students can actually draw and label with letters, scribble writing, or words. Older students sometimes are more engaged if they are also encouraged to include a sketch or small drawing. Consider an interest survey in this format (see Figure 2.2).

The four squares may or may not be used by most of your students. However, you can encourage students to talk about the different types of writing they like to do, including subgenres. For example, a student may like to

Figure 2.2
What Different Kinds of Writing
Do You Enjoy Doing?

I am interested in …	I am interested in …
One experience I had was …	One experience I had was …
I remember this writing piece/project because …	I remember this writing piece/project because…
Does this writing connect with something else you enjoyed doing or will do again?	Does this writing connect with something else you enjoyed doing or will do again?
I am interested in …	I am interested in …
One experience I had was …	One experience I had was …
I remember this writing piece/project because …	I remember this writing piece/project because …
Does this writing connect with something else you enjoyed doing or will do again?	Does this writing connect with something else you enjoyed doing or will do again?

engage in informational writing. He could enjoy the writing process or how-to pieces, as well as writing recipes or want ads. Students can complete the four squares by filling in one, two, three, or all four squares. Looking at this survey provides teachers with knowledge about students' experiences with varying genres, their interests and comfort levels, and their sense of writing identity. How is this knowledge helpful for teachers and students? This survey gives students a chance to think about what they like, what they are good at, and what their writerly lives have been like in the past. It gives teachers an opportunity to discover the writers before them and begin to imagine a plan to nurture these writers and help them grow.

In Figure 2.3, Keller uses all four squares to reflect on the kinds of writing that stood out for her. She has fond memories of her fourth- and fifth-grade writing experiences because these were learning experiences for her. Presenting to the class (specific audience) and illustrating her writing (posterboard ad) made these two pieces memorable. In the final two entries—argumentative and fairy tales—the same two reasons appear again. In the argumentative block, Keller notes that she had to "use a lot of research to support my argument." This was a learning experience for her. In the fairy tale block, Keller says that her sister drew illustrations. We see that writing for Keller takes on an added dimension when she can use illustrations. We also learn from the four

Figure 2.3
Grade Six Four-Square Interest Survey (Keller)

Keller

What different kinds of writing do you enjoy doing?

I am interested in... Persuasive writing

One experience I had was... in 3rd grade when I first learning how to write a Persuasive writing piece.

I remember this writing piece/project because... we had to make a poster board that looked like a ad for a product.

I am interested in... informational/biographics

One experience I had was... in 4th grade when I had to write a biography and I chose Taylor Swift.

I remember this writing piece/project because... I had to present my biography in front of the whole class.

I am interested in... Argumentitive writing

One experience I had was... a couple of months ago in 6th I made a argumentitive about musical training.

I remember this writing piece/project because... I had to use a lot of research to support my argument.

I am interested in... Fairy tales

One experience I had was... in 2nd grade at my house I wrote a lot of my own fairy tales.

I remember this writing piece/project because... I made a lot of fairy tales and my sister would draw the illustrations.

square that Keller values trying out new types of writing. All of this information is important for her writing teacher to know. Keller is an artist; she likes to draw; she likes to try out new things. Tapping into Keller's interests as she chooses topics and researches them, not only aids in motivating writing by appealing to specific audiences but also gives her teacher the opportunity to demonstrate new approaches and genres.

In Figure 2.4, Alyazia completes just two of the four squares, but what she says is revelatory. She expresses interest in writing argument pieces because her experience turned out to be her "favorite piece of the year." Following up with Alyazia to discover what made it her favorite (she enjoyed discovering that research was useful in augmenting her claim) led to steering Alyazia toward selecting topics for informational writing in which she could make use of authentic research. Teachers must know not only what students are interested in but also what motivates them to write, to learn, and to take risks as writers. Student writers who enjoy sharing their writing with others usually note this preference on their four squares as well.

Interest surveys also help students to generate topics for written pieces and may serve as tools for teachers during topic conferences. Sometimes, teachers can use these surveys to form small-group conferences to meet students' needs

Figure 2.4
Grade Six Four-Square Interest Survey (Alyazia)

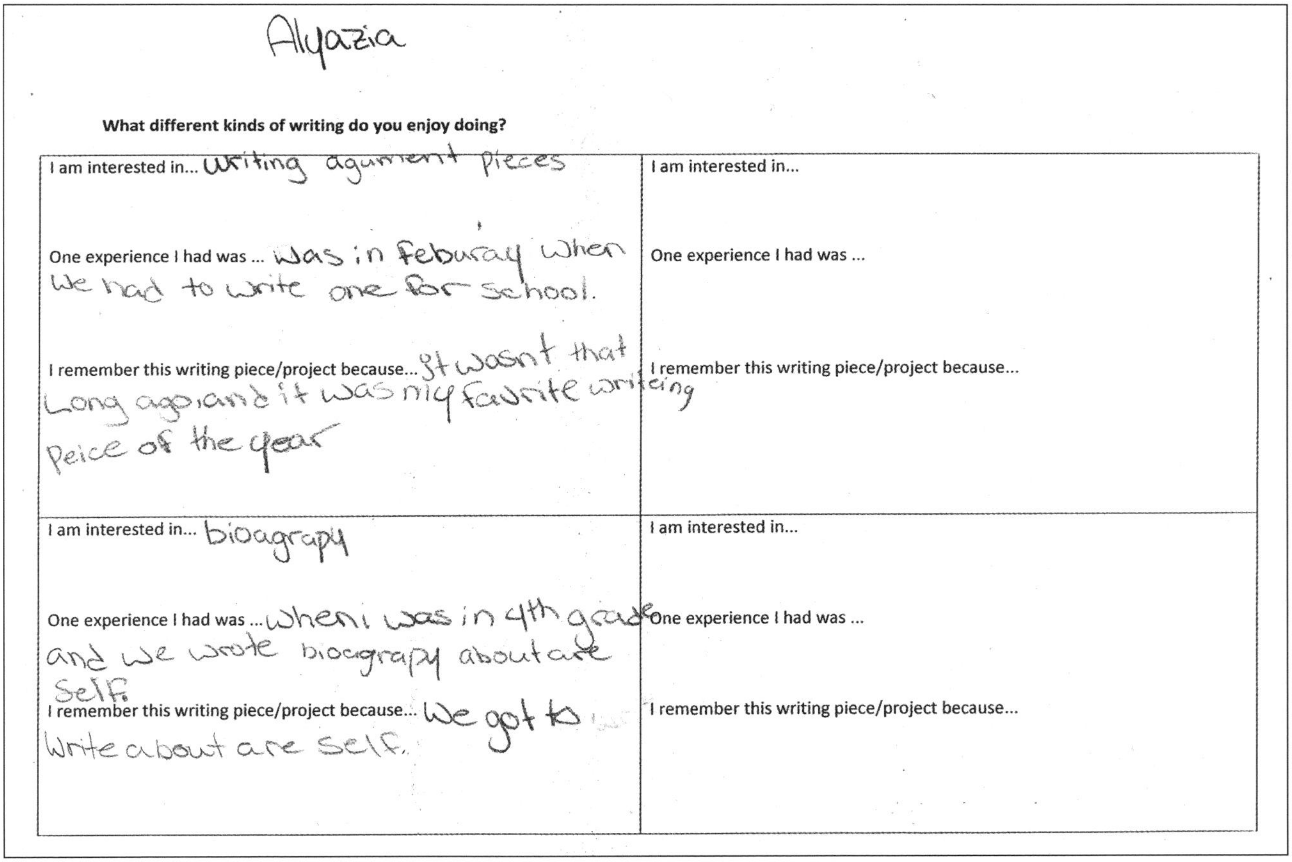

Alyazia

What different kinds of writing do you enjoy doing?

I am interested in... Writing agument pieces One experience I had was ... Was in feburay when we had to write one for school. I remember this writing piece/project because... It wasn't that Long ago, and it was my favorite writing peice of the year	I am interested in... One experience I had was ... I remember this writing piece/project because...
I am interested in... bioagrapy One experience I had was ... when i was in 4th grade and we wrote biography about are self. I remember this writing piece/project because... We got to write about are self.	I am interested in... One experience I had was ... I remember this writing piece/project because...

and to differentiate instruction. A typical writing interest survey might ask these questions:

- Circle the kinds of writing you like to do
  Notebook entries   Stories   Information   Opinion
- Outside of school, how much do you write every day?
  A lot   Sometimes   Almost never
- Something I know a lot about and can write about is . . .
- What are your favorite things to do outside of school?
- What do you like most about writing?
- What do you like least about writing?

SPOTLIGHT ON FORMATIVE ASSESSMENT

First, Take a Learning Stance

When we use formative assessment, we take a learning stance first, as opposed to a teaching stance. I am most often reminded of this whenever I visit kindergarten and first-grade classrooms. I was recently asked to work in a school so that teachers could watch some primary conferences in action. Several teachers and I visited Shelley's kindergarten classroom, where writing workshop was up and running: her students knew the rituals and routines for developing of ideas, illustrating and writing their own books, and holding themselves accountable for all they knew about writing.

I met five-year-old Hannah that day, and she reminded me of the importance of maintaining a learning stance. I walked up to her while she was working on her book about her cat. "Hi, Hannah! What are you working on?"

"My book about my cat."

She proceeded to read me the first two pages, where she included details in pictures and words about things her cat liked to play and where her cat liked to sleep. She was proud to show me that she included speech bubbles on the page about where the cat liked to sleep.

"What are you working on right now in your cat book?" I asked.

"I'm thinking," she responded.

"Okay. So how can I support you?"

"I need time."

Here is where I began to realize that Hannah really needed time more than any kind of advice. But, for some reason (perhaps because four teachers were watching the conference!), I tried again. "Do you want to look again at some of the pages you have done to see if you might add details?"

"No," Hannah quickly replied. "I need time to think. Alone."

I finally "got it." "Oh!" I said. "So you want me to leave you alone so you can think and finish your book!"

"Yes," Hannah replied. She seemed relieved.

She happily shared her completed book with me later in that class period, but this one quick conversation with Hannah shows how important it is to take a learning stance first. Clearly, Hannah had everything she needed as a writer: She had a great idea, and she was excited to continue. She was trying out speech bubbles, her illustrations were full of details, and she was writing words she knew automatically and stretching out other words.

Hannah is a writer. She needed time to work at that moment; she didn't need me. That's because Shelley, her teacher, had provided both strong teaching and time to practice.

When we are truly engaged in formative assessment, we need to watch for these kinds of "Hannah" moments—when kids need time to practice more than they need our feedback. I would argue that, even though I walked away and let Hannah work, I did provide feedback: I was giving her the message that she had everything she needed to get her work done that day. I noticed what she needed at the moment, and what she needed did not include my interruption.

Because of confident writers like Hannah, regardless of the age of student I am working with, before a conference, I ask whether they would mind conferring with me about their writing. About 10 percent of the time, they say: "Can you come back later? I am working right now."

Thanks, Hannah, for making me a better teacher. Perhaps we really do learn everything we need to know in kindergarten.

Mark Overmeyer has worked for more than twenty years in Cherry Creek Schools near Denver, Colorado, as a classroom teacher in grades two to six, a special education and Title I teacher, and a coordinator for gifted programming. Mark's book on conferring is *Let's Talk: Managing One-on-One, Peer, and Small-Group Writing Conferences* (Stenhouse).

Finding Out About Our Students' Attitudes Toward Writing

In a September 2000 article in *Reading Teacher* entitled, "Measuring Attitude Toward Writing: A New Tool for Teachers," Dennis Kear et al. (2000) discuss an attitude survey instrument designed to help teachers discover how to help their students be more successful and joyful writers. Their twenty-eight-item writing attitude survey (WAS) uses four distinct Garfield images, ranging from very happy to very upset to record student responses to questions about writing. The authors explain the procedures for administering the survey and discuss how data were collected. However, the most important feature of the survey is not necessarily the resulting data; it is that such data may be used and should be used to plan instruction. When we teachers know our students as writers, when we know their likes and dislikes, their successes and perceived failures, we are better prepared to provide needed support and specific, focused lessons to help our writers grow.

In March, students in Shelly Keller's kindergarten classroom were asked to respond to a question concerning attitudes toward writing in a whole-class share. They were asked, *Do you like to write?* Lynne and Shelly recorded their thoughts. Some of the responses Lynne wrote down in her writer's notebook were revealing.

Giuliana: I like when we share on little sticky notes whatever we like to write about.

Liam: I like writing nonfiction books because they're true facts and have pictures on every page.

Grace: I like to try new things like similes.

Giovanna: I like to make books with words and pictures.

Zaire: I like to listen to the books my friends write.

Leah: I like writing in my notebook because it's fun.

Keagan: I like to write about people we care about.

For kindergarten through second-grade students, a simple attitude survey can be read aloud to them. Two or three columns with graphics will help students place a check mark in the appropriate column. Early in the kindergarten year, the teacher may want to record the responses during a one-on-one conference and probe to find out more. For example, if a student does not think she is a good writer, it would be helpful to find out why she thinks so to help her build confidence and writing self-esteem. This question also probably relates to how easy or difficult it is for the student to write. If a student in kindergarten is not writing because she does not know how to write any words, then model for her and for the class the importance of scribble writing, with or without letters, and drawing illustrations.

In Kevin Black's third-grade class, Diane used a survey to determine students' attitudes about writing (see Figure 2.5; also available online at sten.pub/acloserlook).

Figure 2.5
My Feelings About Writing

Name _____	**Date** _____		
	☺ Yes	😐 Sometimes	☹ No
1. I like to write.	_____	_____	_____
2. I write at home.	_____	_____	_____
3. Writing is easy for me.	_____	_____	_____
4. I like to write stories.	_____	_____	_____
5. Writing is fun.	_____	_____	_____
6. I like to write nonfiction.	_____	_____	_____
7. I like to share my writing.	_____	_____	_____
8. Writing is boring.	_____	_____	_____
9. I am a good writer.	_____	_____	_____
10. I like to write opinions.	_____	_____	_____

Consider the following two survey responses. The first survey completed by Addison (Figure 2.6) shows a positive attitude toward writing. Addison likes to write, sometimes writes at home, regards writing as "sometimes" easy, and likes everything else about writing: stories, nonfiction, and opinions, as well as sharing writing. Most important, Addison considers herself to be a good writer. Compare her survey to Jim's (Figure 2.7) who admits to having negative feelings about writing. All of his responses are "no" with the exception of "Writing is boring" to which he most emphatically replies, "yes."

Jim's survey expresses entirely negative feelings about writing. Clearly, Jim is going to require much nurturing during writing workshop. Often, what teachers see as obstinate behaviors (not being prepared for writing workshop, staring out the window, writing a sentence or two and saying, "I'm done") are actually an outward manifestation of the fear of writing. Conferring with Jim about topics—what he is interested in, what he likes to do in his spare time, perhaps, even taking dictation as Jim talks about his weekend—can help him recognize that he has interesting and important ideas. Knowing that Jim dislikes or maybe even fears writing informs our instruction. It is important for us to know our writers. In Jim's case, care must be taken not only to help him choose an appropriate topic but also to provide positive feedback to his attempts.

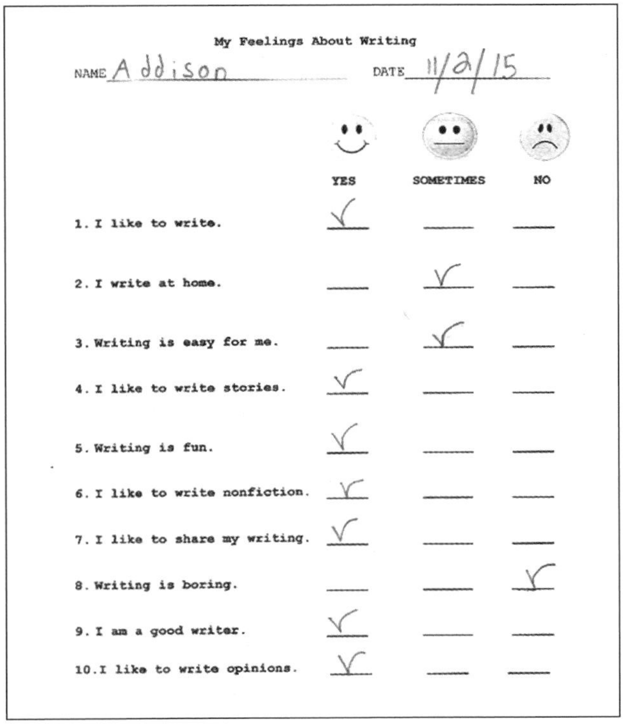

Figure 2.6
My Feelings About Writing (Addison, Grade Three)

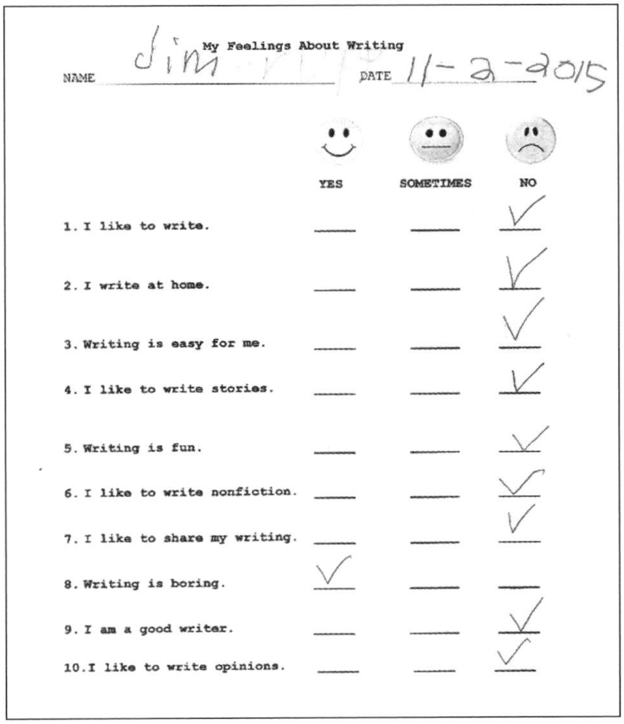

Figure 2.7
My Feelings About Writing (Jim, Grade Three)

What can we do with such surveys? When Diane compiled the results, she had a conversation with Kevin, the students' teacher. Most of the students had positive feelings about writing; however, sixteen of the twenty-two students had mixed feelings about sharing their writing. Fourteen out of twenty-two students had mixed or negative feelings about writing opinions, while twelve of the twenty-two students had mixed or negative feelings about writing nonfiction. Students feelings about sharing were particularly troubling. We can learn much about student progress, as well as students' ability to be good conference partners, by observing their behavior during the sharing portion of the writing workshop.

As Diane conversed with Kevin, she suggested that sharing begin with praising an aspect of the writing. For example, when Allison shared her piece about Halloween, Diane praised her specificity: Allison did not just write *candy* but specified *KitKat*; she didn't just write *dark street* but *an inky sidewalk on Jefferson Avenue*. Emphasize the good things about a piece of writing: "You helped the reader picture the kind of candy and maybe even taste it, Allison." Specifying what works in the piece provides helpful feedback to the writer. Positive and targeted feedback helps the rest of the class, too, since such feedback can help the other students become better conferrers and writers as they try to replicate their classmate's successful technique.

Diane asked Kevin to think about other ways he could help his third graders become more comfortable with sharing, thus becoming better responders to one another's writing. Together, they came up with these ideas:

- Work with a partner of choice or a partner who is writing in the same genre or at about the same level in the writing process.
- Use the author's chair as a special place for students to share their writing.
- Ask students to share their favorite sentence, part, or word and explain why they chose it.
- Allow students to draw sketches with their writing or to use a storyboard to plan a narrative and share the artwork instead of the words.
- Link the sharing with a recent focus lesson to demonstrate the tracks of the teaching and to allow the student to use the thinking on an accompanying anchor chart to help him verbalize.
- Encourage more opportunities to write collaboratively and share as partners or small group.
- Think outside of the box. Ask students to act out (perform their writing).
- Play music in the background during sharing time to help create a mood. During Halloween, students often write haunted house stories. Dim the lights, sit in small circles to share, and give the writer a flashlight to read his piece.

- Give students a chance to practice reading their pieces. Use a tape recorder, or a smartphone, or an iPad Voice Record Pro app so that the students can hear how they sound.
- Train the student peer group/audience to give specific praise. Create several anchor charts with a sample narrative, an informational piece, an opinion piece, and a poem that can be used as models for responding with praise. (They can learn how to give specific feedback on how to polish a piece at a later date.)

Students in Kevin's class made suggestions, too. Here are a few that stood out:

- Practice reading with a partner before sharing. (Owen)
- Share at your table (small-group share). (Jacob)
- Wear an author's hat. (Alex and Ethan)
- Use a megaphone so everyone can hear. (Micheaela)
- Have someone else read your piece to the class. (Milani)
- Show your piece under the visualizer as you read it. (Addison)

These suggestions indicate that at least some of the students, while willing to share their writing, hesitate to do so publicly. Noting which students suggest a smaller-group setting to share is important for a teacher to know. We recognize that much learning, both for the writer and for the listeners, can occur during sharing time. Listeners learn how to be good responders. They may also discover how their classmates have implemented a craft lesson. Writers hear their classmates' reactions, get praise and suggestions, and discover what worked in their piece; therefore, they are likely to try that craft technique again. They also learn which suggestions make sense to use. Writers are decision makers.

Finding Out About Our Students' Engagement Levels

Often, in writing workshop, we meet students who are reluctant to write. They may have decided that they do not like writing or that they are not good at it and never will be good at it. These writers sit in our classrooms every year. If we don't find out about them early on and help them establish a writer's identity, these students will be the same ones who leave us in June as reluctant and struggling writers. Our goal for writing workshop participation is total immersion in the writing process. Students cannot be joyful if they are only compliant. Students who are engaged can find the joy in growing as a writer, trying out new strategies and genres, and sharing their writing with myriad audiences. To help our reluctant or struggling writers as early in the year as possible, we suggest an engagement inventory. It may look something like Figure 2.8:

1. Is [student's name] writing during workshop time? If not, what is he doing?
2. Does this student write at other times across the day when there is opportunity to do so?
3. Does the student find the best spot in the room where he can concentrate while drafting?
4. Is the student working alone all or most of the time or with a partner? When is he more comfortable?
5. Is she "reading the room" (using environmental print) for help with spelling?
6. Does the student stop writing when she is trying to spell a word to wait for help before writing anything else?
7. Does he page through writer's notebook entries to reread or add to a list (for example, expert list, heart map, writing territories, words that describe a season)?
8. Is he producing the same amount of writing most of the students in your class are able to do? More? Less? Explain.
9. Does she do any prewriting? If a plan is developed, is it used?
10. Does he confer with a partner?
11. Does she move closer to an anchor chart to make use of it?
12. How does this student spend his time in workshop? Drawing pictures for a writing piece? Reading a mentor text? Reading for research? Revising drafts and editing pieces of writing? Staring out the window? Using the bathroom? Sharpening a pencil? Reading his independent reading book? (Circle all that apply.)
13. Does the student move on to other writing activities when the draft is finished? If not, what does this student choose to do?

Figure 2.8
Writing Inventory for Engagement

After collecting information for the engagement survey from your observations, you can make good decisions about how to help your student. For example, if your student is having difficulty putting words on paper, he may be experiencing *terror of the blank page*. The more a struggling student stares at his blank paper while everyone around him is pouring out sentences and turning pages or adding a picture, the more terrified or frustrated he will become. Here, writing to the X may help. Simply place a large X one-third of the way down the page (or even less than that) and ask your student to write to that point on the page for that day. During the week or weeks that follow, move the X down the page. For our youngest students, writing fluency is more important than form or correctness. If your student needs a trip to the bathroom or a walk around the room, perhaps he actually needs a whisper partner to share ideas with or needs to orally rehearse the story or poem he is about to write. Providing clipboards for all students is a way to help them move around and still write. Many students have trouble sitting at their desks for long periods. Perhaps you could consider writing a home and school grant or talking with your principal about the possibility of purchasing some standing desks that also have a movable pedal to swing. These desks are adjustable and allow students to stay in one spot and move at the same time. Continue to use this survey to understand your students' needs and to find ways to engage them during workshop time.

When you are creating a survey, you need to know what kind of information you want to get from it. If you have only a vague idea of what you're trying to find out, your questions will be vague, too, and so will your answers. It is always a good idea to put your questions in a logical, meaningful order and to group together questions on similar topics. Easier questions should come earlier in the survey. This makes it more pleasant for your students to take the survey, which increases the likelihood that they will actually finish it in a thoughtful manner or give detailed responses if there are places to write comments. If you give the survey orally, this also will help build rapport with the student, especially in the beginning of the school year when the student is still feeling new and unsure of teacher expectations. However, the more difficult questions should be placed near the end of the survey. If students see a tough question right at the beginning, for all they know, all the questions could be that difficult and filling out the survey starts to look like a real chore. But if they see it at the end, they may put in the effort because they know they're almost done, or because by this point (if you are administering the survey orally) they like you and trust you. Even if they do not finish, at least you will have most or half of a survey to analyze, instead of none. This advice goes not only for difficult questions but also for sensitive questions that ask students how they feel about writing.

Creating a Survey to Gain Knowledge of Skills or Genre

Surveys can serve other purposes, too. In Karen Drew's fourth grade, Lynne began an informational writing unit of study with a survey to find out what the students knew about how to gather research. Students were reading biographies in order to write a focused informational piece around a "secret," something most readers would not know about the famous person, so Lynne asked the fourth graders to think about how they might find information to write about someone like Benjamin Franklin. Lynne asked the students what they already knew about Franklin. Some fourth graders thought he had been a United States president and a few thought he wrote the Declaration of Independence. Many students knew about his experiment with the kite and a key. Lynne had just shared Frank Murphy's *Take a Hike, Teddy Roosevelt!* (2015), so she used this book to place Franklin on a historical time line. Lynne queried, "Franklin lived during the time George Washington was a general in the American Revolution. We'll put him on the time line before Teddy Roosevelt was even born. We can't interview him, so how could we write a picture book biography about him?" She asked the students to create a list in their writer's notebook. She asked them to call the list *How to Begin Research After You Have a Topic* and to turn and talk with a partner after they had at least three ideas on their list. Lynne surveyed the students by asking them to exchange journals and to share their partner's ideas. As they shared, she asked the writers to raise their hands if the idea appeared on the list their partner created so she could tally them. The following chart (see Figure 2.9) gave Lynne and Karen ideas for immediate future focus lessons. They could see at a glance what most kids

Sources for Research	Tallies of Votes
books at the library	⊤⊤⊤⊤ ⊤⊤⊤⊤ ⊤⊤⊤⊤ ⊤⊤⊤⊤ ‖
magazines	⊤⊤⊤⊤ ⊤⊤⊤⊤ ‖‖
newspapers	⊤⊤⊤⊤ ⊤⊤⊤⊤ ⊤⊤⊤⊤ ‖‖‖
photographs	⊤⊤⊤⊤ ⊤⊤⊤⊤
museums (the Franklin Institute)	⊤⊤⊤⊤ ⊤⊤⊤⊤ ⊤⊤⊤⊤
the house where born or lived	⊤⊤⊤⊤ ‖
journals, diaries, letters, notebooks, postcards	⊤⊤⊤⊤ ⊤⊤⊤⊤ ⊤⊤⊤⊤ ⊤⊤⊤⊤ ‖
paintings, sketches, sculpture	⊤⊤⊤⊤ ‖‖‖
family members (descendants)	‖‖‖
articles of clothing or a craft (lace doily, hand-painted china, shawls, dresses, breeches, boots, shoes)	‖‖‖

Figure 2.9
Assessing Student Knowledge
About Sources for Research

talked about and understood and what could be included to help these young writers gather interesting ideas for their informational project.

The one they chose to do the following day concerned back matter—what you find at the end of a book, such as an afterword, an author's note, an epilogue, a glossary, or a fact sheet. These sections of back matter inform the reader about some aspect of the book. Back matter can vary, and choices largely depend on what each particular book needs. Karen and Lynne searched for several picture book biographies with back matter and came up with *Enormous Smallness: A Story of E. E. Cummings and His Creative Bravery* by Matthew Burgess (2015), *Mr. Ferris and His Wheel* by Kathryn Gibbs Davis (2014), and *On a Beam of Light: A Story of Albert Einstein* by Jennifer Berne (2013). Each mentor text presents different kinds of back matter. For example, Burgess's book contains a chronology, an author's note, acknowledgments, and even a few poems by E. E. Cummings. However, in Davis's book, you can find the sources for the quotes that are used, websites, a bibliography for further research, and a photograph. Back matter is a great source to extend inquiry and to be able to write something new instead of just repeating what most people already know. The survey was one way of getting at what the fourth-grade writers knew about how to conduct research and what might significantly add to their investigative powers.

In addition to surveys and inventories, teachers may also employ brainstormed lists, such as expert or authority lists. Mark Overmeyer (2005) provides an overview of a number of ways to help students who "don't know what to write about" (21–33). In one sixth-grade classroom, Diane modeled authority lists for the students as one option for finding topics for writing. An authority list includes topics a student feels he knows a great deal about or would like to learn more about. Often, these expert lists lean toward nonfiction writing ideas but not always. Consider the following three authority lists from a sixth-grade class.

Notice the detail in Alex's list (Figure 2.10).

Alex has specific details within the categories. She isn't only listing names but has notations to remind her of what she can write about. She also has topics that lend themselves to information or even opinion writing: fishing with her dad, for example, could be an informational piece about how to fish in a lake or in the ocean. She plays right forward on the soccer team. She might

Figure 2.10
Authority List (Alex, Grade Six)

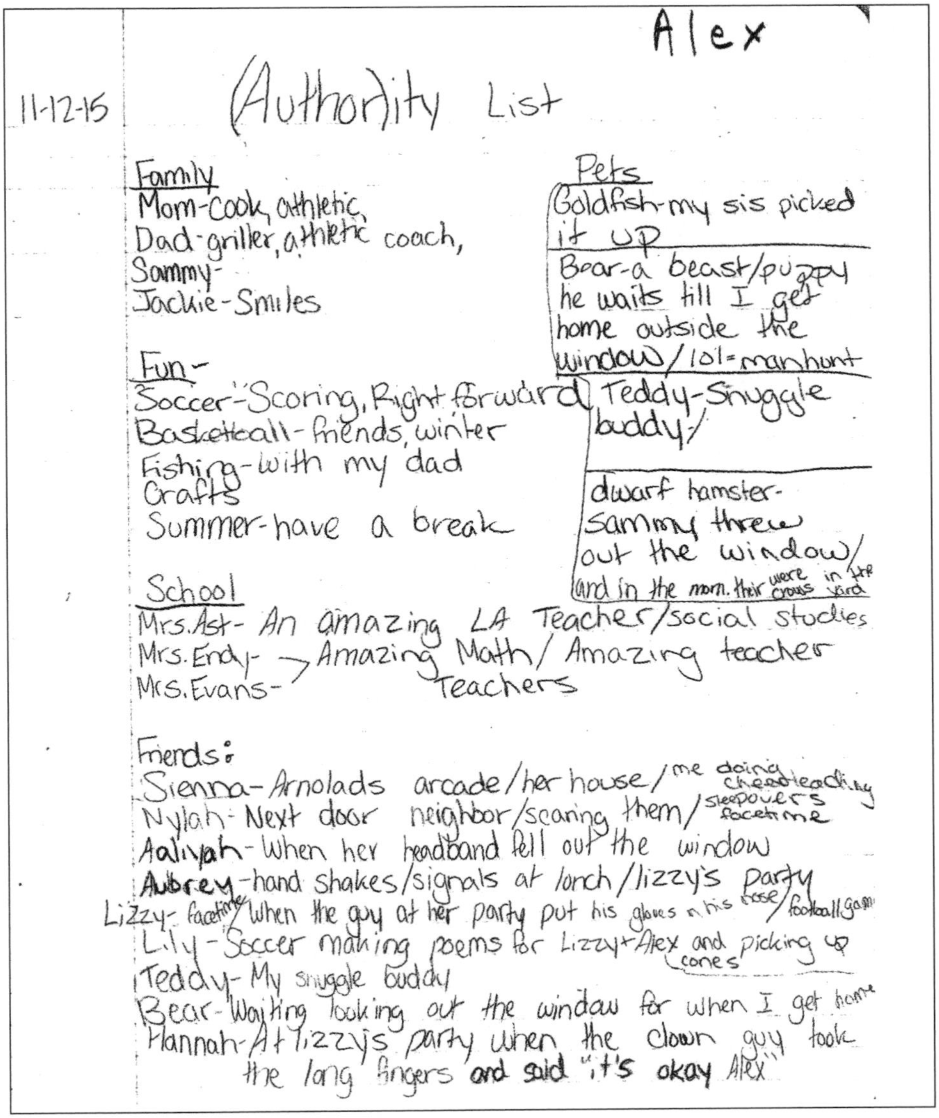
Alex

11-12-15 (Authority List

Family
Mom-Cook, athletic,
Dad-griller, athletic coach,
Sammy-
Jackie-Smiles

Fun-
Soccer-Scoring, Right forward
Basketball-friends, winter
Fishing-with my dad
Crafts
Summer-have a break

School
Mrs. Ast- An amazing LA Teacher/social studies
Mrs. Endy- Amazing Math/ Amazing teacher
Mrs. Evans- Teachers

Friends:
Sienna-Arnolads arcade/her house/me doing cheerleading
Nylah-Next door neighbor/scaring them/sleepovers facetime
Aaliyah-When her headband fell out the window
Aubrey-hand shakes/signals at lunch/lizzy's party
Lizzy-facetime/when the guy at her party put his gloves n his nose/football game
Lily-Soccer making poems for Lizzy+Alex and picking up cones
Teddy-My snuggle buddy
Bear-Waiting looking out the window for when I get home
Hannah-At lizzy's party when the clown guy took the long fingers and said "it's okay Alex"

Pets
Goldfish-my sis picked it up
Bear-a beast/puppy he waits till I get home outside the window/101=manhunt
Teddy-Snuggle buddy/
dwarf hamster-Sammy threw out the window/ and in the morn. their were crows in the yard

write an informational piece on how to play right forward or an opinion/argument about soccer being the best sport to play. Alex doesn't just list the names of her pets but lists characteristics that she can use to help her plan a narrative piece.

Amanda's list is less detailed but contains a great deal of useful topic-generating ideas (Figure 2.11): Under *Family* she does add some descriptors, but for the other categories, she does not. In a quick conference with Amanda, Diane asked specific questions to help Amanda flesh out her lists, particularly the *Sports* and *Injuries* categories. Is Amanda on a school or an athletic association team? Are the injuries related to her playing sports? What small moment or moments with her friends come to mind?

Figure 2.11
Authority List (Amanda, Grade Six)

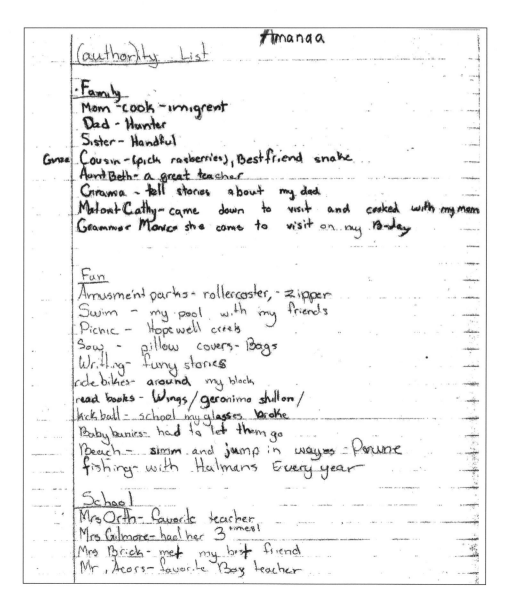

Figure 2.11
Authority List (Amanda, Grade
Six) *(continued)*

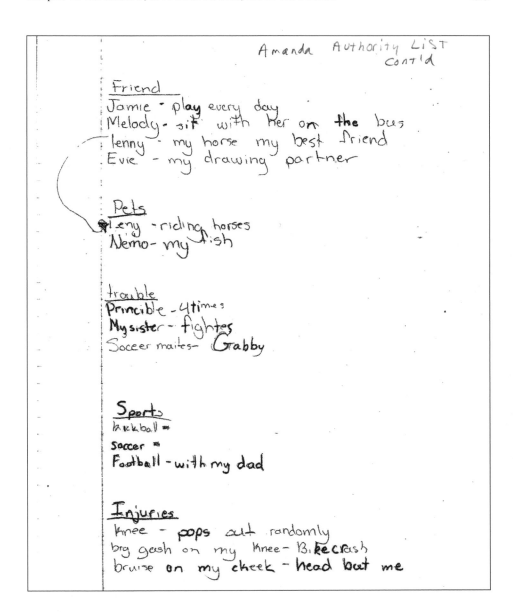

Amanda   Authority List
                    cont'd

Friend
Jamie - play every day
Melody - sit with her on the bus
lenny - my horse my best friend
Evie - my drawing partner

Pets
lleny - riding horses
Nemo - my fish

trouble
Princible - 4times
My sister - fightes
Soccer maites - Gabby

Sports
kickball =
Soccer =
Football - with my dad

Injuries
knee - pops out randomly
big gash on my knee - Bike crash
bruise on my cheek - head but me

Jack's list is minimal (Figure 2.12). What does his lack of content show the teacher? Does it mean Jack is uninterested in writing? Does it mean he needs more time to think? Does it mean he doesn't believe he has anything interesting to write about? Only through conferring with Jack can we know the answers to these questions. Taking time to help student writers complete topic-generating lists and surveys during writing workshop is time well spent. As we model our own lists and as we peek over the shoulders of our student writers, we learn a great deal.

Figure 2.12
Authority List (Jack, Grade Six)

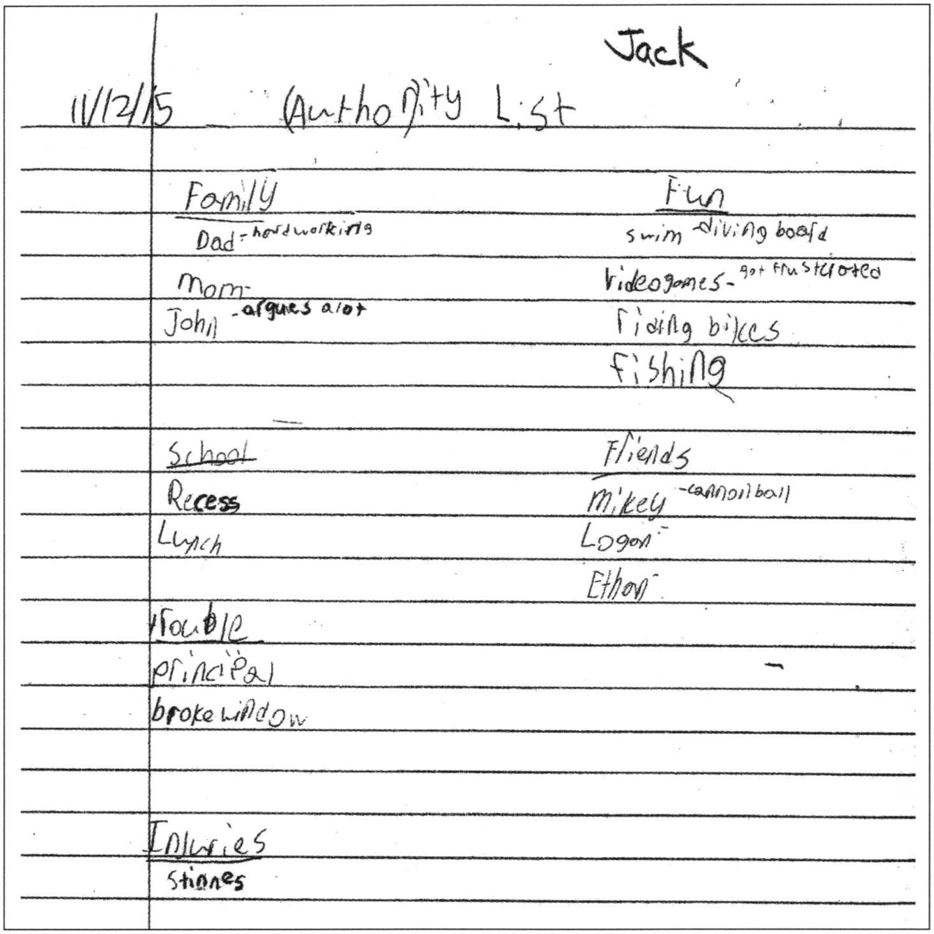

Jack

11/12/15 Authority List

Family
Dad - hardworking
Mom -
John - argues alot

Fun
swim - diving board
videogames - got frustrated
riding bikes
fishing

School
Recess
Lunch

Friends
Mikey - cannonball
Logan
Ethan

Trouble
principal
broke window

Injuries
stiches

Letters from Parents: A True Gift

A great way to get useful information on each child even before you begin the school year is to write a letter to your students' parents. Lynne wrote a letter of introduction each year asking her parents to write a letter in response, sharing anything about their child they thought might be important for Lynne to know. She asked them to tell her about their child's reading habits, special interests, and if they wrote or draw at home. Lynne suggested that they share something their child seemed to enjoy from the previous school year or something the child was looking forward to this school year. She included a self-addressed stamped envelope to make things easier for the parents. Although she never received a letter from each household, she often received more than half. Today, parents can send an e-mail, but there are other challenges, as the number of English language learners increase in our classes. One year, Lynne left notepaper on her students' desks at open house and asked parents to take a few minutes to write a few things they thought she should know about their child. The next year she left a stamped postcard at each desk, urging parents to take the postcard home; jot down some things they thought she should know about their child's interests, successes, and fears; and drop it in the mail. Sometimes, she encouraged them to share at the first conference and jotted a few notes. If parents were not comfortable with sharing, that was okay, too. Seeking help from parents strengthens the community and helps us get a clearer picture of the students we greet each September. In his chapter "Vision and Choice in the K–3 Writing Workshop" in *Write Now! Empowering Writers in Today's K–6 Classroom*, Matt Glover's simple strategies can help teachers guide students to find topics to write about. He suggests talking with parents about their child's interests. Matt says, "I'm often amazed when I find out that a student has an interest that I didn't know about, especially when I thought I knew the student well" (Glover 2014, 66). Letters can offer surprising, important insights into a child's interests, attitude toward reading and writing, and expectations for the coming year.

Our Final Thoughts

Surveys and inventories are easy to create, to administer, and to evaluate. Surveys, inventories, and letters may also help to build and maintain a learning community. As writing teachers, the more we know about how our students feel on the inside, the better equipped we are to help them to become better writers on the outside. The written products they create and we read and respond to do not occur in a vacuum. We need to be aware of what our students need from us. As we plan our writing lessons, we recognize where our students are and where we can take them. Formative assessment is the vehicle through which all of this is possible.

Chapter 3

CHECKLISTS AND RUBRICS

> The idea that students will learn better if they know what they are supposed to learn is so important! . . . The most powerful way to share with students a vision of what they are supposed to be learning is to make sure your instructional activities and formative assessments . . . are performances of understanding.
>
> —Susan Brookhart, *How to Create and Use Rubrics for Formative Assessment and Grading*

Each new school year is a new beginning for teachers and their students. Writing workshop may look different from year to year, depending on the students themselves, their experiences, their attitudes, and their abilities. Nevertheless, procedures from year to year will likely remain the same. Those shiny faces looking up at you in September expect to be taught; they expect to be listened to and honored; they expect the opportunity to express themselves. We owe it to our students to be ready to help them move forward as readers and writers. When we make a commitment to writing workshop, we recognize that students need the chance to write every day, to practice, to self-evaluate, and to share what they are learning about writing with others.

One procedure that has remained constant in our writing workshops is including checklists for student and teacher use throughout units of study. For example, when students are composing narratives in the beginning of the year, they shouldn't have to guess about what is expected of them. They shouldn't have to wait until they have completed the piece to receive feedback or to self-assess. Students need guidance throughout the unit of study. When we provide them with checklists, we are giving students a vehicle for self-assessment. We are also providing ourselves with a tool we can use to monitor and adjust our teaching. We can use the checklists to record which students need targeted instruction, which students need just a nudge or push, and which students are ready to move on.

Getting Ready to Write

Checklists are a way to help students plan their pieces. As the name implies, a checklist is a compilation of items necessary for successful completion of a task. As a shopping list contains items one wants to be sure to purchase on a trip to the grocery store, a writing checklist contains items to be included in a piece of writing.

We want students to think before they write, to plan a course of action, and to use that plan to develop a topic in their unique voices. The following checklist may help student writers in that regard (Figure 3.1).

Figure 3.1
Getting Ready to Write

Steps to Get Ready to Write	Check Here	Notes: Words, Phrases, Drawings, Graphic Organizers
My topic size is just right		
I have something to say		
I have words to bring the reader with me		
I have some pictures in my head		
I have decided how to organize it		
I know where to find information		

Student writers can use this checklist to write out or draw their narrow topic and big idea, for example. This checklist is not meant to be prescriptive or limiting. Instead, it should free students to approach their pieces with confidence that they have chosen a topic that works for them. Teachers can use the checklist in roving conferences to guide students in their attempts. For younger students, such as kindergarteners and first graders, it may be helpful to create this checklist on a larger sheet of paper with three boxes on the top and three boxes below to allow more space for drawing and making notes.

Narrative Checklists

Checklists can be used in the revision and editing stages as well. They also can aid in trying a new approach and in helping students to reflect on the decisions they make as they develop their writing pieces. A narrative checklist, for example, might look like Figure 3.2 (also available online at sten.pub/acloserlook):

Figure 3.2
Narrative Writing Checklist

Narrative Name_____ **Writing Checklist**

My narrative includes the following craft:

It has a lead/hook:
____ Weather lead ____ Snapshot of setting ____ Snapshot of character
____ Action/suspense ____ Dialogue or thought shot

A combination of effective craft:
____ Appeal to senses ____ Exploding moment ____ Splash of dialogue
____ Vivid adjectives ____ Strong verbs ____ Precise nouns
____ Show, not tell

It has a clear focus:
____ It is about one thing. ____ All the details are needed.

It has a clear organization:
____ It has a time order.

A satisfying ending:
____ Action ____ Final thought
____ Hope, wish, or dream for the future ____ Lesson learned

A reader will find my story easy to read:
____ I have used complete sentences.
____ I have used commas purposefully.
____ I have checked my spelling, underlining words I am not sure about.
____ I have indented for each new paragraph.

For a checklist to be effective, student writers need to know how to use it. Terms need to be understood by all the students. For example, before students can check what kind of lead they think they used, they need to have had craft lessons modeling these leads. Teachers may reduce the choices in any category, depending on the lessons they are using during writing workshop, how much of the school year has lapsed, and student writers' experience using the various elements. The important thing is to provide ample choice and significant instructional time, not only to the craft lesson but also to the application of the craft lesson. Once students know all the aspects of the checklist, they will be able to use it effectively.

Teachers can use checklists as formative assessment, also. As we circulate and confer during writing workshop, we record student progress or lack thereof. As students use their checklists, we notice what they are doing and what they merely think they are doing. Allie checks that she has used a *snapshot of setting lead*. Her narrative begins: *We were in the mall shopping. My mom and brother and I went to Aero Postal and spent $81.39.* Clearly, Allie needs further instruction in what constitutes a snapshot of setting. The checklist aids the teacher in assessing what Allie actually can do.

Checklists can be designed for each genre or type of writing students are doing. As you design a checklist, focus on the essentials. What do students need to do, and why do they need to do it? In the narrative checklist, the inclusion of five kinds of leads and three kinds of endings indicates that the creator of the checklist wants students to recognize the importance of leads and endings in a narrative piece of writing, and that the students need to choose a lead and ending that will fit the story. Other skills of importance include focus and organization, as well as grammatical concerns that make the piece easy to read. The design reflects the teacher's lessons and explores student achievement of the goals of these lessons.

A Checklist for Writing Arguments

In the following checklist for argument writing, Diane focused on the lessons she and Kris Endy, the sixth-grade teacher, decided were needed based on the students' knowledge and understanding of writing an argument. Argument writing is sophisticated, requiring students not only to formulate an opinion but also to back up that opinion with reasons based on evidence. As an introduction to the argument writing unit, Kris and Diane asked students to define argument writing. After reading examples of argument pieces, the teachers led the class in a discussion of what constitutes an effective argument. Their responses demonstrated that, though students knew the difference between a fact and an opinion, they were not convinced that facts can support opinions. They needed to have a clearer understanding of terms; they needed to know how to use evidence to support their claims. An anchor chart developed with the class that named the components of an effective argument became the basis for a checklist and rubric students used as they drafted and revised their pieces.

Breaking the unit into focus lessons, followed by monitoring individual student competencies in applying those lessons to their writing, allowed Kris and Diane the opportunity to provide one-on-one, small-group, and whole-group instruction to move the writers forward as they composed their pieces. The checklist (Figure 3.3; also available online) acted as a reminder to students of the focus lessons as they completed their work. Because the checklist asks students to comment on their own pieces, it may also work as a self-evaluation for conferring.

Claudia writes on her checklist that she is most proud of her research: "It was really hard in the beginning because I needed to remember to check the

Please check all that apply and write a comment below about what you think are the strengths of your argument piece.

The piece is written for a specific audience. _____

I clearly stated my opinion. _____

I found facts to support my opinion. _____

I took notes and used my own words or used quotation marks when I used the author's words. _____

I made a list of my sources. _____

I included the "other side" (counterargument). _____

The piece has a clear beginning, which states the opinion in a thesis statement. _____

Each body paragraph begins with a reason that supports the thesis statement. _____

Details, examples, explanations, and facts support each reason and do not sound like a list. _____

The conclusion summarizes the piece and provides a convincing restatement of the point statement and the main ideas that support it. _____

The writing sounds like me. It has my voice. _____

What are the best parts of this piece? What are you proudest of? Comment in the box below.

Comment here:

Figure 3.3
Revision Checklist for
Argumentative Writing

source on the Internet." She also writes that sharing the argument with the class was "fun because we could ask questions." Jamie says that "writing the thesis statement was the best part. I was proud that I could do it and that my argument made a point." Looking at the checklists along with the pieces informs the teacher not only of what the student writer can do but what he thinks he can do. Used in the revision stage, the checklist also guides the teacher in one-on-one conferences and roving conferences.

Help with Informational Writing

An informational writing checklist (Figure 3.4; also available online) that sixth graders used in the spring helped them to self-assess their pieces before meeting for one-on-one conferences with their teacher. Kris asked the student writers to list the ways they added content to their informational pieces in addition to checking off the items on the checklist. Mini-lessons and mentor texts emphasized the use of facts, definitions, concrete details, and anecdotes. Students checked to ensure they used three of the four strategies to add content to their informational pieces.

Please check all that apply and write a comment below about the strengths of this informational piece.

Is the piece written for a specific audience?   _____

Is my topic not too narrow or too broad?   _____

Does the piece have an introduction, a body, and a summary or a conclusion?   _____

Does the introduction have a strong point or purpose statement stated in a positive way?   _____

Does each body paragraph begin with a reason that supports the point statement or purpose?   _____

Do details, examples, explanations, and facts support each reason and not sound like a list?   _____

Does the conclusion summarize the piece and provide a convincing restatement of the point
    statement and main ideas that support it?   _____

Does this writing sound like me? Did it have my "voice"?   _____

I included the following in my informational piece (at least three). I highlighted examples in my paper.

____ facts   ____ definitions   ____ anecdotes   ____ descriptions

____ concrete details (details that are specific to the topic, using content specific vocabulary)

Figure 3.4
Revision Checklist for
Informational Writing

Figure 3.5
Characteristics of Effective
Writing

Creating a Checklist with Your Students

Sometimes, a teacher can create a checklist with or without the help of the students. Of course, if the students are involved in the creation of the checklist, they will have ownership and will be much more likely to use it for peer assessment and self-assessment. Here is an example of a student checklist that may be useful for looking at writing characteristics (Figure 3.5; also available online):

Name _____   **Date**_____   **Grade**_____

Focus
____ I am aware of my audience.
____ My purpose is clear.
____ I write from one point of view.
____ My ideas are clear.

Content
____ My details support the topic.
____ My information relates to the focus.
____ My ideas are fully developed.

Organization
____ My writing is in a logical sequence.
____ Each paragraph sticks to one subject.
____ I move from one point to another logically.
____ I have a good beginning and ending.

Style
____ My language is clear and precise.
____ My choice of words is good.
____ My language is fresh and original.
____ I use a variety of sentence patterns.

Conventions
____ My spelling, capitalization, and punctuation
    are correct.
____ My grammar is correct.
____ My sentences are complete.

Placing checklists like this one on Google Drive helps students and teachers with quick, easy access, depending on the grade level of your students and the availability of computers, laptops, and iPads to use on a regular basis. Their value is also in the ability to make changes—revision or editing—and share these documents across the grade level and in lead teacher teams or even in professional development sessions.

SPOTLIGHT ON FORMATIVE ASSESSMENT

Oral Rehearsal Provides Opportunities to Practice

One of the most helpful tools I have used to gauge a writer's understanding of my expectations of her during a given day's writing workshop is oral rehearsal. Oral rehearsal provides the writer with the opportunity to practice, or rehearse either on her fingers, in her mind, or with a peer, what she would like to write, before she sets off to work independently.

Before a writer would stare at a blank piece of paper, unsure of what to write, providing him with time to practice what he would like to say offers the writer feedback to successfully accomplish the task. Likewise, it gives the teacher a glimpse into his understanding of the mini-lesson and the writing task he needs to complete. For instance, when a writer is being charged with choosing the best organizational style for her topic, if she is provided with the opportunity to practice verbally what she thinks she wants to write, the teacher can determine whether she understood the task, was able to choose an appropriate structure for her writing, and provide feedback before she commits to writing through that structure. Moreover, for writers who struggle with remembering from the carpet to their desk what they were asked to write, oral rehearsal is an additional means through which working memory can be activated.

Especially when crafting arguments and counterarguments, and determining whether the evidence the writer is providing is appropriate to support the claim, or refute the counterargument, oral rehearsal can allow the writer to run through his ideas, measure their effectiveness, and determine whether they are weighty enough to prove the writer's point. When done with peers, oral rehearsal can provide the writer with feedback and ideas they may not have thought of on her own. The teacher can listen in to the conversation and reexplain, reteach, or confirm effective writing moves well before the teacher gets a chance to read the writer's work—before she needs to ask the writer to explain her thinking more clearly or to rewrite (and even re-research) to eliminate weak evidence.

Through oral rehearsal, the teacher and writer can focus on refining craft and improving the level of writing, instead of having the writer start on the wrong track, only to be brought back to start anew. The teacher and writer can accomplish more when this version of formative assessment is put into place during the brainstorming process.

Aileen Hower is a K–12 literacy/ESL supervisor for South Western School District in Hanover, Pennsylvania. In this role, she serves as a literacy coach who models writing workshop lessons for elementary-level teachers.

What About Rubrics?

Rubrics, though typically used for summative assessment, can be a formative assessment tool as well. A rubric is a coherent set of criteria for student work (in this case, a piece of writing) that describes levels of performance quality. Unfortunately, rubrics are not as simple as they may look. They are hard to create, sometimes difficult to use, and commonly misunderstood and misused. We think of rubrics as a collaborative effort devised under the direction of the teacher but with significant student input. Suppose, for example, that third graders are writing an opinion text-based piece. We discuss with the class the qualities of an effective opinion. We share mentor texts, such as *Groundhog Gets a Say* by Pamela Swallow (2005); *A Fine, Fine School* by Sharon Creech (2001); *Red Is Best* by Kathy Stinson (1960); *The Perfect Pet* by Margie Palatini (2003); and *One Word from Sophia* by Jim Averbeck (2015). We share teacher- and student-created pieces and help students to decide what works well in the piece. As an example, *The Perfect Pet* begins with a catchy opening: "Elizabeth really, really, *really* wanted a pet," that clearly states Elizabeth's point of view. Her parents' point of view is equally emphasized: "Her parents really, really, *really* did not." As the story progresses, Elizabeth tries various efforts to achieve her objective. As a class, the third graders decide on the qualities of a good opinion piece of writing.

- The opinion is clearly stated. (A _____ would be a good pet)
- Reason for choosing this pet. (_____ would be a good pet because)
- Example of why this is a good reason (This pet could work in this family in this way)

These qualities become the basis for our rubric in addition to the qualities of good writing intrinsic to any successful piece of writing (ideas, organization, word choice, sentence variety, and conventions). With the third graders' input, Diane and Kevin designed a rubric for opinion writing (Figure 3.6; also available online).

How can student involvement in creating a rubric inform our instruction as we work with students who are writing opinion pieces? We notice and keep a record of which students are contributing to the rubric design and which students need clarification. We recognize students' needs by watching closely as they confer with a partner and jot notes in their writer's notebooks. This information guides us as we engage students in the unit of study. Add missing information to a rubric that you and your students identify. You can also decide to omit criteria as well. A rubric is only useful if it fits your students' work in writing workshop and across the day.

In *How to Create and Use Rubrics for Formative Assessment and Grading*, Susan M. Brookhart (2013) discusses the essential components of effective rubrics: criteria that relate to the learning and not to the tasks that students are

	Focus	**Ideas**	**Organization**	**Word Choice**	**Conventions**
4 - Great	My opinion is stated clearly. It is easy to recognize my opinion.	I explain how each reason supports my opinion by using clear facts and details.	I have an introduction and a conclusion. I explain one reason at a time to make sure my opinion makes sense and use transition words and phrases to connect the reasons.	I used specific words and phrases to explain my opinion. My words relate to my topic and clearly show what I think and what I believe.	I edit my paper for spelling, punctuation, and capitalization. There are few, if any, errors.
3 - Good	I state my opinion.	I give more than one reason for my opinion.	I have an introduction and a conclusion. I use my reasons to organize my paper. I sometimes use transition words to connect reasons.	I used some specific words to explain my opinion. My words relate to my topic. The reader knows what I think about my topic.	I edit my paper for spelling, punctuation, and capitalization. There are some errors, but the reader can tell what I am trying to say.
2 - Okay	I have an opinion, but it is hard to find it.	I give at least one reason for my opinion.	My reasons are not explained in any particular order. My paper might not use transition words.	I used a few specific words to explain my opinion. My words sometimes show what I think.	I try to edit my paper. There are errors in spelling, punctuation, and capitalization that may make my paper hard to read in spots.
1 - Needs Work	My opinion is not stated. My readers may be confused.	My opinion is not supported by reasons.	My opinion is hard to follow because my reasons aren't in order. My paper is missing an introduction, a conclusion, or both. I do not use transition words.	My words are general and could apply to different topics. I do not clearly show my thinking.	I had trouble editing my paper. Readers may not understand my paper because of the errors in spelling, punctuation, and capitalization.

Figure 3.6
Rubric for Opinion Writing Grade Three

asked to demonstrate, and explicit descriptions of performance across a continuum of quality. In addition, Brookhart outlines the difference between various kinds of rubrics and explains when each type of rubric may be appropriate. Ayres and Shubitz (2010) discuss online rubric makers such as Rubistar but caution teachers that this may not be the best approach. Instead, creating rubrics together with your students is ideal for raising their understanding of what the criteria are and ensuring they are doable. Student samples can be used as mentor texts to give a concrete picture of what students should be looking for in a particular genre. Creating a rubric with your students will take some time, but it makes them an integral part of the assessment process.

A valuable source for rubrics is *Creating Writers: 6 Traits, Process, Workshop, and Literature* (sixth edition) by Vicki Spandel (2012). Spandel honored the work of Paul Diederich and his team for inspiring the six traits. His Diederich scale can easily be found by searching "Diederich Scale for Raters of Writing" under Google Images. In *Learning by Teaching*, Donald Murray (1982) identified six traits: meaning, authority, voice, development, design, and clarity. Whatever terms are used to describe the characteristics of writing, the important thing is to understand each one. For example, what does *voice* mean and how is it achieved in a piece of writing? Placed on a rubric, these six qualities, or traits, can be used to discuss what the writer has done or might be able to do. Here, the terms are useful so that everyone is using the same nomenclature. In a conference, it is crucial to be able to discuss students' progress toward existing goals and setting new ones. The rubric can be a formative assessment tool, not necessarily used to establish a final grade.

In the appendixes of *Creating Writers*, Spandel gives both teachers and students a great gift. Appendix 2 (Spandel 2012, 435–437) offers teachers a three-level writing guide to sort writers into 1–2, 3–4, and 5–6. This grouping is very freeing and buys the teacher precious time to organize groups of writers for small-group conferences and additional mini-lesson work. Appendix 3 (Spandel 2012, 438–439) is designed for the students in this same way. Students can use this three-level guide to assess the work of a peer or for self-assessment—offering to help in revision and editing or setting new goals for future pieces of writing.

Checklists for Conferring and Feedback

Brenda Krupp, a third-grade teacher, created a simple, effective checklist to display on her writing center bulletin board so that her students could readily refer to it during peer conferences (see Figure 3.7). As she created this anchor chart with her students, she urged them to think about the two roles they play: the reader (the writer who creates a text) and the partner (who listens carefully to ask questions or to motivate). The students suggested drawing an arrow from the questions a partner asks to changes the reader/writer may decide to make

Figure 3.7
How to Confer with a Partner

to strengthen their piece. These questions often relate to FARMS: *focus, add, remove, move, substitute.* Brenda's class offered these strategies to writers based on questions they had received during peer conferences:

1. Focus—Know who your target audience is.
2. Add—Add details to support your big ideas: description to help your reader use his senses, develop setting and characters; dialogue to create voice; exploding a moment in time where the reader should feel he is there with you; a simile to anchor an important idea.
3. Remove—Remove sentences that take the reader off track and weaken the focus of your piece. Take out clichés and replace them with original thoughts.
4. Move—Move words, phrases, sentences, or even paragraphs to logical and meaningful places. Make sure everything is in the perfect place.
5. Substitute—Look at your nouns and verbs. Change them up if they are not strong and specific. Take out lazy sentences that don't say much, and create new ones with action and vivid detail.

The poster is a subtle way to nudge student writers to make some changes to their pieces after a conference or, at the very least, to consider doing some revision work. An additional poster to use as a checklist titled *Farm It!* for revision work, created by Susan Powidzki, a librarian at Upper Moreland School

District, reminds students to revise their writing using *focus*, *add*, *remove*, *move*, and *substitute* as areas to consider. (See Figure 3.8a and 3.8b; also available online.)

Figure 3.8a
Farm It!... A Revision Check

Figure 3.8b
FARMS Mini-lessons for Revision

FOCUS: modes (awareness), narrowing the topic, choosing a topic, point (*so what?*), target audience, point of view, purpose, topic appropriate for age level

ADD: color, size, shape, similes, metaphors, appeal to the senses, anecdotes, emotions, thoughts, details, statistics, snapshots of setting and character, vivid adjectives, opinions, wow facts, examples, explanations, different types of sentences, proper nouns, description of setting, the power of three, alliteration, quotes from the experts, statistics

REMOVE: redundancy, pronouns if possible, clichés, overworked words and expressions, overabundance of similes and metaphors or ones that do not work well with the piece, information that dims our focus

MOVE: order of words, phrases, sentences, and even whole paragraphs to make the piece more logical, meaningful, and powerful; move adjectives after the noun they describe to create rhythm and variety; move the movable *-ly* adverbs and prepositional phrases to create new ways to begin sentences

SUBSTITUTE: replace weak language with strong verbs, exact nouns, and vivid adjectives to help create pictures in our readers' minds; replace language that does not sound like you (takes away your voice) and rephrase in your own words and voice.

Checklists to Help with Conferring and Record Keeping

Checklists are useful during a conference in several ways. They help the teacher record notes, sometimes by simply circling points on the checklist. Later, a teacher can look through the notes and information checked to create a new list of teaching points for mini-lessons. Another way to use this information is to look for similar needs to create small-group conferences or small, flexible groups for instruction. (See Figure 3.9; also available online.)

Figure 3.9
Qualities of Writing Conference Notes

FOCUS
- What's the topic?
- What's the point?
- Does the writer stick to the topic and the point?
- Does the writer stray?
- How precise is the point? Does it control the content?

CONTENT
- What ideas does the writer present?
- Are there too many ideas?
- Has the writer chosen quality ideas?
- How much elaboration is included—a lot, some, a little bit?

ORGANIZATION
- Is there a beginning, a middle, and an end?
- Did the writer include an opening sentence and a concluding sentence?
- Are the ideas grouped together logically?
- Is the order meaningful?
- Does the author move from one idea to the next smoothly?
- Are there transition words to help the reader move from one idea to the next?

STYLE
- Did the writer use strong verbs, exact nouns, and vivid adjectives?
- Did the author use a variety of sentence structures?
- Did the author try to start his sentences different ways?
- Are there are a variety of lengths of sentences?
- Did the author use figurative language?
- Does the writer know who his audience is?
- Does the author set a mood or a tone with writing that sounds like him?

GRAMMAR & CONVENTIONS
- What risks in punctuation did the writer take?
- Did this writer try something new with sentence structures or word placement?
- What errors interfere with the reader's understanding?
- Did the writer experiment with new learnings from class instruction in conventions and/or parts of speech (such as using prepositional phrases to begin sentences)?

Fletcher and Portalupi (2001) suggest using different-colored checklists to accommodate the skills levels in your classroom. They suggest keeping a one-page sheet where you can see all of your students at a glance for tracking skills your students have mastered. Whatever you choose to use, keep it simple so you will be able to use it with confidence and ease.

Another interesting checklist helps the teacher circle strengths or weaknesses in a two-column checklist that highlights both process and product. Teachers can simply use two different colors to denote strengths and weaknesses. Another way to use this checklist is to look only at process or at product (see Figure 3.10; also available online).

Figure 3.10
Teacher Checklist: Process and Product

Name _____	**Date** _____

Product	**Process**
1. Does it have a focus? • Awareness of audience • Clear purpose 2. Presence of quality ideas 3. Ideas are developed • Examples • Descriptions • Anecdotes • Quotes from the experts • Statistics • Dialogue • Explanations 4. A meaningful organization • Uses variety of leads • Transitions are appropriate • Text structures are apparent • Variety of conclusions • Use of paragraphs 5. Style • Specific word choice • Sounds like the writer • Sentence variety 6. Conventions • Punctuation • Capitalization • Spelling • Spacing between words • Uppercase and lowercase FURTHER COMMENTS:	1. Evidence of prewriting • Outline • Sketch • Notes • Graphic organizer • Freewrite 2. Evidence of multiple drafts • Writing fluency • Changes made as a result of conferring 3. Revision • Additions • Deletions • Removing redundant content • Removing clichés • Moving words, sentences, paragraphs • Substitute for stronger verbs and nouns 4. Editing • Presentation—formatting, eligibility, reader ready 5. Demeanor • Listening skills in conferring • Asking good questions • Worthy suggestions FURTHER COMMENTS:

Teacher Checklists to Help Think About How Writing Workshop Is Working

To keep important components of writing workshop in mind, you may use the following checklist as a self-assessment tool or ask a colleague or literacy coach to observe your workshop in action and fill in the grid two or three times in a school year. The months can be changed or added. A quick look can say much about your growth as a writing teacher and how your writing workshop operates. (See Figure 3.11; also available online.)

Figure 3.11
Components of Writing Workshop

Components of Writing Workshop	**September**	**November**	**January**
Use of stages as recursive encouraged: planning/prewriting, drafting, revising, editing, publishing, sharing			
Literature models used as mentor texts in mini-lessons, conferences, or part of the reflection discussion			
Modeling by teacher, samples from literature/mentor texts, and/or student samples			
Conferences (teacher-student as formal or informal, such as roving conference, whole group, small group)			
Peer response groups or peer conferring with partners			
Long, daily chunks of time for writing, individually or collaboratively			
Gives choice of writing topic and freedom to abandon and start anew			
Use of well-timed, compact mini-lessons and longer *Your Turn* lessons			
Formative assessment and self-evaluation: anchor charts, anecdotal records, status of the class, conferring notes, discussion observations (circle all that apply)			
In the table above, place **I** = ideal, **A** = acceptable, and **N** = not yet.			

We also suggest that teachers maintain a checklist to document their growth and understanding as a writing teacher. Perhaps some questions such as the following will work for you. You may want to use this checklist to record your thoughts in a journal and discuss them with a colleague or in a grade-level meeting.

- The time allotted for writing workshop is just right.
  (If I think it is too long or too short, how can I adjust the internal workings to make it a better fit?)
- I have varied writing supplies (paper, markers, etc.) that students can easily access themselves.
  (What supplies do I think should be available for students?)
- The students' writing shows the tracks of my teaching.
  (What can I do if my students' writing does not show evidence of the strategies I am teaching them?)
- I have a place to display my students' writing that includes work in progress.
  (If I don't display work in progress, how do I honor student attempts?)
- I give all steps of the writing process about equal attention.
  (If I spend too much time in editing for publication, how can I change that?)
- I create units around craft moves and process and the three writing types.
  (If this is not the case, can I adjust my yearly schedule to fit in opportunities for author study, poetry, and attention to craft moves?)
- I recognize that it is important for my students to share their struggles and their successes.
  (Sharing our struggles can be very important. It is here that students notice and note problem-solving strategies and appropriate them for their own use. What problems am I noticing that my students are encountering?)
- The student writing sometimes reflects individual choice that is independent of assigned writing.
  (Do my students have opportunities to create graphic works, poems, and so on at different times throughout the year?)

As teachers, we continually reflect on our own practices to become better teachers today than we were yesterday.

Our Final Thoughts

Formative assessment practices help us see the holes in a student's writing history—the missing pieces we need to fill in so they can grow in sophistication and confidence during the school year. Landrigan and Mulligan (2013) state that formative assessment is all about finding these gaps between the knowledge (in this case, the knowledge about writing strategies, skills, and craft moves) that students use and the gray areas where improvement is possible with instruction, support, and reflection. Both teacher and student benefit from an understanding of the gaps that exist and can work together to fill them. Checklists and rubrics help us recognize the gaps in a timely manner, so we can do something about them.

Chapter 4

ANCHOR CHARTS
A Record of Student Thinking and Evidence of Progress

> How can we "hold thinking"—making it both permanent and visible? When planning, I need to think through not only what I want kids to know, do, and understand, but also how *both* of us will know what they know.
>
> —Debbie Miller, *Reading with Meaning: Teaching Comprehension in the Primary Grades*

Cris Tovani (2011) in *So What Do They Really Know?* states that she creates anchor charts that synthesize thinking that the students will need to go back to over time. Tovani records not only their thinking but also the name of the student responsible for the thinking. She dates and saves anchor charts to serve as tangible artifacts of learning in the classroom.

Using anchor charts as visible representations of students' thinking helps not only those students who are contributing to the chart but also all students in the class; all students see and can use the information the chart elicits. When we ask students to share what they already know and can do in a unit of study, we allow them to reflect on their prior knowledge. When we ask students to apply what they know or think they know about a facet of writing, both teachers and students are better prepared to engage in a conversation about the writing.

Procedural Anchor Charts

To start the school year with anchor charts, do a procedural mini-lesson on how you can spend your time in writing workshop, especially after completing a piece of writing. Establishing an anchor chart of *Things I Can Do in Writing Workshop* and posting it for all to see avoids two problems: (1) students who are not engaged who disrupt other students and (2) students who spend writing workshop time to catch up on independent reading. Although reading independently is a good thing, we want our students to spend the time devoted to writing workshop doing the work of a writer. Sometimes that involves reading from several sources to gather research for an informational or opinion piece. Most school districts designate less than an hour for writing workshop time (sometimes as little as thirty minutes); therefore, we want to send a message to students that we do not want them to hurry through a writing piece so they can curl up with a favorite book. Students need to understand their options and imagine the possibilities for deeper writing and new writing. In fourth grade, Karen Drew and Lynne created an anchor chart in September to add to possibilities for writing workshop. The original anchor chart contained a few key thoughts, including: begin a new piece of writing, write in your writer's notebook, listen to someone else read his or her work, and have a conference with the teacher. After a few weeks of workshop, the fourth graders added to their anchor chart (see Figure 4.1).

Names of students who shared ideas for this anchor chart were included after each idea. That way, the students were honored for helping the writing community move forward, and Karen and Lynne could see which students were hanging back and not voicing their ideas. Then, it was up to Karen and Lynne to make sure that these quiet students understood the options for a writing workshop period and perhaps to find ways to help them to be comfortable sharing in whole-group situations.

Anchor charts help to make the learning permanent and visible for all to see. Anchor charts are the work of a teacher and her students. This collaboration makes an anchor chart worth the time it takes to construct one. Creating an anchor chart enables us to observe our writers to determine their level of engagement, their productivity and time management, and their ability to operate inde-

Figure 4.1
Things to Do During Writing Workshop

1. *Begin a new piece of writing. (Taryn)*
2. *Write in your writer's notebook. (Kevin)*
3. *Listen to someone else's piece. (Rachel)*
4. *Sign up for a conference with the teacher. (Joslyn)*
5. *Plan for a writing piece (sketch, list, web). (Jayden)*
6. *"Talk" your piece to someone before you begin to write it (oral rehearsal). (Jimmy)*
7. *Have a conference with a partner (praise-polish). (Conor)*
8. *Have a conference with yourself and revise! Read your piece out loud. (Gianna)*
9. *Add to your "Expert" list. (Nigel)*
10. *Read books to find more research for your topic. (Jimmy)*
11. *Try to practice a new craft move by adding it to a piece of writing. (Erin)*

pendently (Do they refer to an anchor chart for options? Do they need more direction?). An anchor chart also keeps students from forming a long queue at the teacher's desk or designated conference area. Students should be working on other pieces, rereading, or drawing pictures, diagrams, or time lines for their pieces, but they should never be standing in a line waiting for a conference.

What happens when student writers suffer from writer's block? In Brenda Krupp's third-grade class, students had a writerly conversation about getting into a "block" where you can't seem to get unstuck or put down your ideas on paper in the way you want it to go. Brenda asked her writers to gather on the rug to turn and talk about possible solutions to a question that had been troubling some students for a long time. She felt that an anchor chart would help move these students with strategies to use to get unstuck and help her know whether most of her students had a plan of action when they couldn't move forward with their writing. The students suggested the following in an anchor chart labeled:

What Do Writers Do When They Get Stuck?

- Abandon this piece for now and start a new piece.
- Wait until the next day to work on this piece again.
- Return to your plan or prewriting and revise.
- Take a bathroom break so you can walk through the hall and get your mind thinking.
- Read other pieces in your writer's notebook to find ideas.
- Use your notebook to study craft moves that might help you.
- Meditate—breathe in and out—until you are relaxed.
- Sketch it out, draw pictures, or use a storyboard.
- Write about something that makes you happy.
- Write about something that makes you sad.
- Talk to a classmate or two about your problem to get help.
- Return to some mentor texts to get a new idea to write about.
- Ask yourself questions: *Who? What? Where? When? Why? How?*
- Close your eyes and think.

This anchor chart served as a reminder to student writers that there are many ways to get yourself unstuck, and if one doesn't work, simply try another.

Anchor charts are useful for formative assessment. Observe how your students use the anchor charts. Do you see students moving closer to the chart to reread and think about the information the class has posted? Do students continue to add new thinking to these charts? As a teacher, how do you honor this new thinking? Do you ask students to initial their contributions? Do you revisit the charts from time to time to assess students' understanding of key ideas and their practical application?

Another procedural anchor chart helps students develop the art of question-making as a writer and a responder. Often student writers have difficulty asking questions of themselves or others to move a piece of writing forward. They never know what to ask. Diane worked with third graders to demonstrate the importance of asking writers good questions to help them draft and revise. She orally told them a story: "The time I fell off the monkey bars at recess and broke my arm":

> *I was in fourth grade and I loved climbing on the monkey bars. Every time we had recess I would run to be first to use them. I was glad to be there instead of math class. I didn't like fractions. The day I fell it was cold and windy. I swung from bar to bar and made it across to the opposite side. Then, I had an idea. "Hey, look at me! I'm going to do it backwards." I put one hand behind me, reached the bar and kept on going. The steel bar was cold and slippery. When I was halfway across, my hand slipped and I fell sideways on my arm. I heard a crack. Then I felt a sharp pain. Everyone came running over. A teacher asked me if I could get up to walk into the school. They called my father, and he took me to the emergency room. My arm was broken.*

Kevin Black, the third-grade teacher, then asked me questions about my story.

Which arm did you break?

What did the monkey bars look like?

Why is it important to know that you were in math class before recess? Do we need to know that you didn't like math to understand what happened in the story?

What was the weather like?

Can you explain some more about how you came to slip and fall?

Why didn't they call an ambulance?

How long did you have to wait in the emergency room?

What year was it?

How will you end this story?

After Kevin asked the questions, Diane explained to the students which questions she would answer and which ones she would not. The emergency room question, for example, would not be part of this story because the story will end with the fall. While the year is not important to the story, Kevin, asking the question about math, pointed out that this detail is also irrelevant. However, asking about the ending helps the writer to think about the point of the narrative.

As part of the lesson Kevin, Diane, and the class developed an anchor chart that categorized questions by type:

Kinds of Questions to Ask Writers

To ask for more information:

What time of year was it?

What happened when you fell?

Who came to help you?

How did it feel when you fell?

What grade were you in?

How tall were the monkey bars?

Which arm did you break?

To clear up something you didn't understand:

What did the monkey bars look like?

How did you fall? Did your hands slip?

Why is it important to your story that you didn't like math?

To ask for examples:

Can you tell me more about the playground equipment?

What did the playground look like?

What can you tell me about the ground around the monkey bars?

To ask about the ending:

How will this end?

How will you know when your story is finished?

Are there details that don't fit now that you have an ending?

Guiding students to recognize questions that help writers to clarify their thinking and to solidify details is an essential facet of writing workshop. The categories of questions can be used for each type of writing although the questions themselves will change. The questions Kevin asked about Diane's story were specific to her narrative. The anchor chart, then, listed only the types of questions and not the specific ones.

Types of Questions to Ask Writers

Questions that ask for more information

Questions to clear up what you don't understand as a reader/listener

Questions that ask for examples

Questions about the ending

Students in Kevin's class used the question anchor chart in the narrative unit of study as a reference to give feedback to students who shared their writing at the close of daily writing workshop. During the informational unit of study, they revisited the question anchor chart, brainstormed questions specific to their shared informational writing, and referred to the chart again during small-group sharing time as they wrote their informational pieces. In observing students during their conferring, Kevin and Diane could assess which students used the chart to formulate questions and which students still needed help developing appropriate questions during a peer conference.

Anchor Charts for a Narrative Unit of Study

Third graders in Brenda Krupp's class gathered as a community to brainstorm possibilities for a *what if* story. Brenda's purpose was to help her students discover topics to write about in which they could fictionalize events in their lives to move them from personal narrative to realistic fiction. Because many elementary school students write more informational recounts than narratives, Brenda thought a *what if* story would help them create real problems, insert tension into their pieces, and solve the problems with satisfying endings in the form of lessons learned. The *what if* anchor chart helped Brenda to assess the students' ability to come up with an interesting problem that was possible to solve realistically. The chart reflects a *what if* topic from every student. First, Brenda referred to *Circus Mirandus* by Cassie Beasley (2015), a recent read-aloud that had become a class favorite. "What could be the *what if* for this story?" Claire suggested, "What if you had to do something very brave to try to save someone you loved?" Students suggested other *what if* questions for *Circus Mirandus*. Then, Brenda asked them to think of some *what if* possibilities for the narratives they would write, to jot some ideas down in their writer's notebook, and to turn and talk with a partner. In whole group, students suggested scenarios, and Brenda asked them to tell her a little more about the problem: how it would affect the main character emotionally and how this problem could possibly be resolved. For example, Mya suggested, "What if your best friend moves to another state?" Her first thought about how to solve the problem of missing a friend so much it hurt was the arrival of a new student in her class who would become her best friend. Brenda encouraged all the students to talk through their *what if* story and to find at least two ways to solve the problem. Mya's second solution was to find a friend at her Saturday gymnastics class. The students were genuinely excited to try this out. Using the chart, each student selected an idea (either their own or a classmate's) or thought of a new idea for a story and listed at least two possible solutions before starting to write. Later that week, Brenda circulated among the class to observe students using the anchor chart for ideas, coming up with new ones, and being able to brainstorm possible solutions for their *what if* stories (see Figure 4.2).

Brenda then asked students to examine sets of picture books to determine a unifying theme for each set. Brenda created an anchor chart based on student labels for the themes they encountered. Her anchor chart helped students cre-

Figure 4.2
Anchor Chart Creating Fiction: What If?

ate narrative, fictionalized stories that ended in a lesson learned. In other words, Brenda was asking her students to start with an understanding of the way their stories would end in order to write the beginning and develop the plot. The themes the students brainstormed for the mentor text sets helped Brenda to recognize what her students understood about the meaning of theme and how the same theme could be applied to different stories. (See Figure 4.3.)

After students had drafted *what if* stories constructed around lessons learned, Brenda gathered the students to discuss revision strategies for their stories. She asked them to come up with a definition of *revision* and Jax volunteered, "Revision is when you make changes for the better." Then, Brenda asked the students to look at their drafts and think about things they might do

Figure 4.3
Anchor Chart Creating
Fiction/Lessons Learned

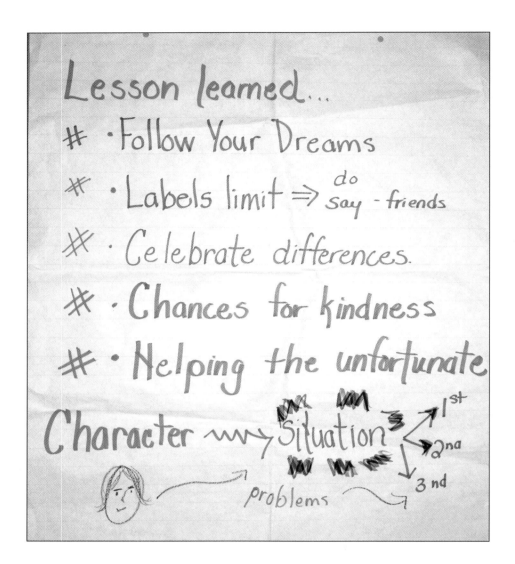

to revise their pieces. The students' suggestions revealed their knowledge of all the traits, as they talked about including specific word choice, creating a sequence of events, remembering to have a focus, or *so what*, using muscular content (variety of detail, description), and thinking about punctuation choices. Brenda encouraged the students to talk about each addition to the anchor chart (see Figure 4.4), even though every idea could not be written there. Dan had offered "revising for better leads." When Brenda encouraged students to talk about this, they brought up trying out more than one lead and then deciding which one best fit their story. Many of them talked about trying a dialogue and an action lead instead of relying on leads they had used repeatedly: the question lead, beginning with onomatopoeia, for example.

Brenda continued to refer to the anchor chart over the next week as students continued to revise, to confer, and to revise some more. She gathered them on the rug and asked them to look at the revision anchor chart. "What

Figure 4.4
Anchor Chart Revision

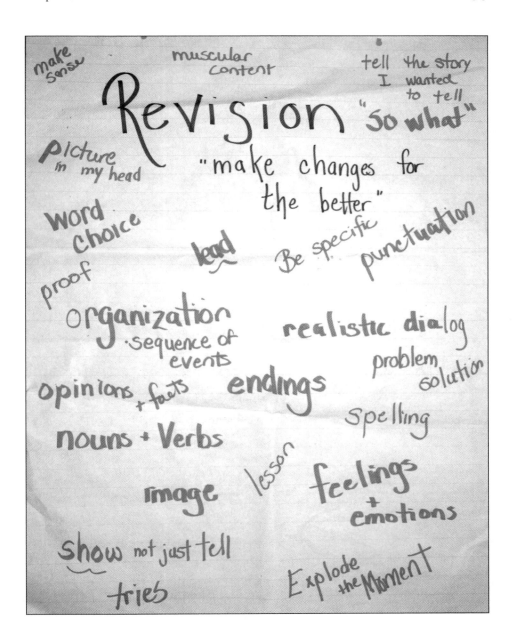

are we missing?" she queried. Brenda charged the students to come up with a revision list that began with verbs that describe their process. Here is the list they created.

Verbs That Tell Our Process

- Show don't tell
- Relive the prewriting experience
- Explode a moment in time
- Persevere when the going gets tough
- Add specific details

- Combine sentences when it works
- Play with words
- Rethink your lead
- Act out an action that is hard to describe
- Take away words and sentences you don't need
- Suggest some changes to a peer in a conference
- Ask questions to help add more details
- Replay the entire story in your mind
- Substitute for stronger verbs
- Skip the parts your story doesn't need

Brenda asked students who still had questions to place them on a sticky note and to attach those questions to the chart. These charts gave Brenda a clear picture of what her students knew about the writing process and revising narratives in particular. The sticky notes informed her of which students needed further instruction.

Anchor Charts for an Informational Unit of Study

In late November, to determine what the students in Kevin Black's third-grade classroom already knew about informational writing, Diane and Kevin began by listing the categories as students recalled them.

What Is Informative Writing?
- FACTS (something that you can prove)
- PHOTOS
- NONFICTION
- USES NONFICTION WORDS
- MAPS AND CHARTS
- EXPLANATIONS
- FEATURES OF TEXT (TABLE OF CONTENTS, CAPTIONS, GRAPHS)
- HAS A BEGINNING, A MIDDLE, AND AN END

Notice that the students know a great deal about features of informational text: maps and charts, graphs, table of contents, captions, diagrams, and photos. Students also know that informational writing deals in facts and explanations. They know that facts are statements that can be proved or disproved. In addition, the student writers agreed that informative writing needs a beginning, a middle, and an end. They seem to conflate informational writing with the entire nonfiction genre, as well as the elements of any good writing piece. Beginning the informational writing unit of study with a list such as this allows both teacher and student writers to recognize what is common knowledge and what needs to be clarified. For example, although all the items the students listed could be used in an informational piece, the third graders decided that they would probably use facts, specific details, explanations, and nonfiction words (the nomenclature of their topic).

Students in the third grade are ready to write about topics that they are interested in and want to know more about; however, they need to be able to consult sources to find enough information to complete their pieces. With the students, Diane and Kevin discussed what qualified as a source. Answers included the Internet, books and magazines, other people (experts), and the library. When students were given a short piece from *Time for Kids* entitled "Wild, Wild Pets" by Suzanne Zimbler (2016) to read in pairs, not surprisingly, information they recorded in their writer's notebooks was copied word for word from the text. "Wild, Wild Pets" discusses that many Americans keep wild animals as pets. The most commonly copied text appeared at the beginning of each paragraph: "Hundreds of thousands of wild creatures are kept in backyards and basements all around the country."

To help student writers use sources without copying word for word, Diane used Nicola Davies's *One Tiny Turtle* as a read-aloud. Students listened to the narrative, talked to a partner about what they remembered, and contributed to a list Diane recorded on a chart.

In *One Tiny Turtle*, Davies (2005) also lists factual information throughout the narrative as secondary text. Instead of reading this information to the class, Diane listed it for the students to view on the visualizer. After each short paragraph, Diane covered the information the students read together and asked them to turn and talk with a partner about what stood out for them, what they thought was important. These important facts were also listed on the chart.

Diane wanted students to recall the facts without having access to the actual words in the piece, because she wanted students to use their own words. Often, when young writers (and some not-so-young writers) use sources, they record the author's story word for word. To get the third graders to practice using their own words, Diane did not provide them with hard copy of the text. Because they had the opportunity to work with a partner or in a small group, and because the information provided was in small bits, the students had little difficulty defining and remembering important facts. When students pursued their own topics, Kevin used the one-book-open-at-a-time strategy. When students were reading, their writer's notebooks were turned facedown. When they wrote facts they remembered, the source was turned facedown while they wrote in their writer's notebooks. As students conferred with Kevin and Diane, they were asked to bring their sources with them so Kevin and Diane could spot-check whether students were paraphrasing.

On the third day, the class participated in a shared-writing experience. The list of information in the anchor chart is only a list. Lists, alone, do not make up an informational piece of writing. Facts are important elements, but to create a coherent piece of writing, facts must be organized. Diane asked the students to turn and talk about how they thought this information should be put together. The life cycle of the loggerhead turtle emerged naturally as the organizational vehicle for the piece.

After the shared writing, Diane and Kevin revisited the questioning anchor chart and, with the students, brainstormed questions they might ask themselves about the shared writing. The students noted that the same kinds of questions they developed for narrative writing also worked well with informational writing. What else do they think readers would like to know? Is there anything that is not clear to the reader? Can the piece use any examples? Does the ending work? The students practiced coming up with questions to prepare to be good responders and self-conferrers as they began to write their own informational pieces.

Molly suggested the question, "If the egg is as big as a ping-pong ball, is it also thin like a ping-pong ball?" Julia thought that the reader might want to know whether male turtles stayed close to shore to help the baby turtles when they hatch. Colson wondered, "Should we give an example of how deep the nest is dug in the sand? Can we compare it to something else?" Gillian asked, "How long does it take for the baby turtles to get to the water after they hatch?" Practicing questioning as a group gave students confidence in formulating their own questions as they produced informational pieces later.

Diane and Kevin then returned to their original informational writing list and helped students revise it, eliminating some details and adding others. (See Figure 4.5.)

Figure 4.5
What Is Informational Writing?

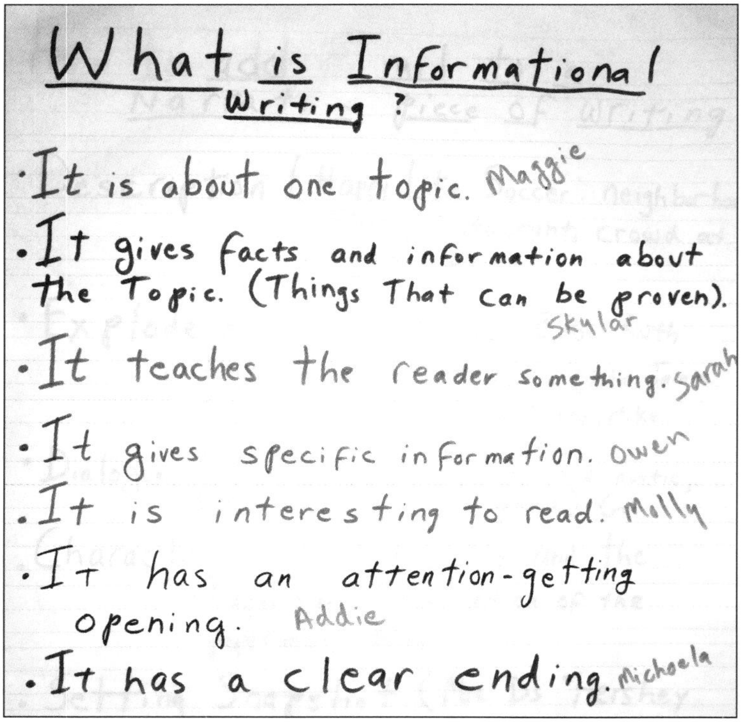

Kevin and Diane allowed the students to keep the final three bullet points even though these features are included in any genre of writing. Student writers need as many reminders of what it takes to produce good writing pieces as they can get. While conferring, Kevin and Diane noted how the student writers had used the anchor chart to grow as writers of informational texts.

Anchor Charts for Sixth Grade

Anchor charts are useful at all grade levels. During a narrative unit of study with sixth graders, Diane began by asking students to define narrative. Though the question may seem elementary, it turns out that the responses were revelatory: students mentioned that it's a story, it has characters, something happens (it has a plot), it is organized in time order, it has a setting, it has details, it uses description, and it makes a point. The list is problematic in several ways. First, though narrative does contain these elements, the elements are not exclusive to narrative. Description and details, for example, are elements of any good piece of writing, including informational and opinion/argument writing. Time order may be used to organize a narrative piece, but there are other sophisticated organizational designs that sixth graders may employ to advance their narratives. The most glaring omission, however, is that not a single student mentioned that a narrative needs a problem or a conflict. Diane probed further to discover that most of the students—accustomed to writing narratives in response to writing prompts or in response to reading—believed that narrative writing is an informational retelling: *What I did on my summer vacation. My week at the beach. Our trip to Hershey Park.* These "narratives" are litanies of *and then . . .* and are not true narratives but simple recounts of events that have taken place either for real or in the student's imagination. In any case, knowing what sixth-grade student writers considered to be narrative informed instruction for the narrative unit at the outset.

Using short text examples, such as picture books, classic short stories, and student- and teacher-written samples as mentor texts, Diane and the student writers developed a new list of elements of narrative writing: hook or lead (attention-getting opening), characters (who), setting (where and when), plot (action), problem/conflict, dialogue (what people say and think), theme (message or point), and conclusion (satisfying ending).

Note the inclusion of not only conflict (problem) but also dialogue, theme or message, hook or lead, and satisfying ending. With this new consensus, students brainstormed possible topics for their narratives. Diane modeled with an authority list of her own that students used to fashion their individual authority lists. (See Chapter 2, "Surveys, Inventories, and Letters.") When students selected their topics, they used the elements of narrative to plan their pieces and to recite the story orally to a partner. Diane and sixth-grade teacher Kris Endy monitored the conversations, specifically noticing whether the storytellers were including the elements of narrative in their rehearsals. *Who were the characters? Where were they? What were they doing? What problem developed? How was the problem solved? If it wasn't solved, how did the situation change?*

Kris instructed a small group of students who needed further teaching in the narrative elements. During the unit, as craft lessons were introduced, students tried them in their writer's notebooks or in their pieces. This also gave Kris and Diane the opportunity to monitor their progress and to reteach whole group, small group, or individually as needed. Early on, it became apparent that students were having difficulty adding detail to their narratives. Telling the bare-bones story seemed sufficient to many of the writers. The class revisited some of the short texts read earlier in the unit, specifically noting where and how the authors added detail. *Happy Like Soccer* by Maribeth Boelts (2014) tells the story of a young girl who plays on a soccer team and wishes that she had someone to cheer for her. Boelts adds detail by way of vivid description: "My shoes have flames and my ball spins on this spread-out sea of grass with no weeds, fields with no holes, and real goals, not two garbage cans shoved together like in the lot by my apartment, where soccer means any kid who shows up to play." Description is also specific, showing the neighborhood by portraying its features: "We weave past the empty lot and through my neighborhood and outside the city, where the buses don't run" (Boelts 2014). Students looked at the text through the visualizer, noting other passages filled with description. Then, they went back to their narratives to add detail through vivid description. Diane began an anchor chart with the class entitled *How to Add Detail to a Narrative*. Vivid description (*Happy Like Soccer*) became the first entry on the anchor chart. As craft lessons ensued, students added to the anchor chart. (See Figure 4.6.)

Students used the anchor chart to return to examples in the classroom library as they continued writing their narratives. They also added examples to the chart as the unit of study progressed, such as *In November* by Cynthia Rylant for rich description, "The Tell-Tale Heart" by Edgar Allan Poe to explode a moment, and "The Cask of Amontillado," also by Poe, for character snapshot.

Figure 4.6
How to Add Detail to a Narrative

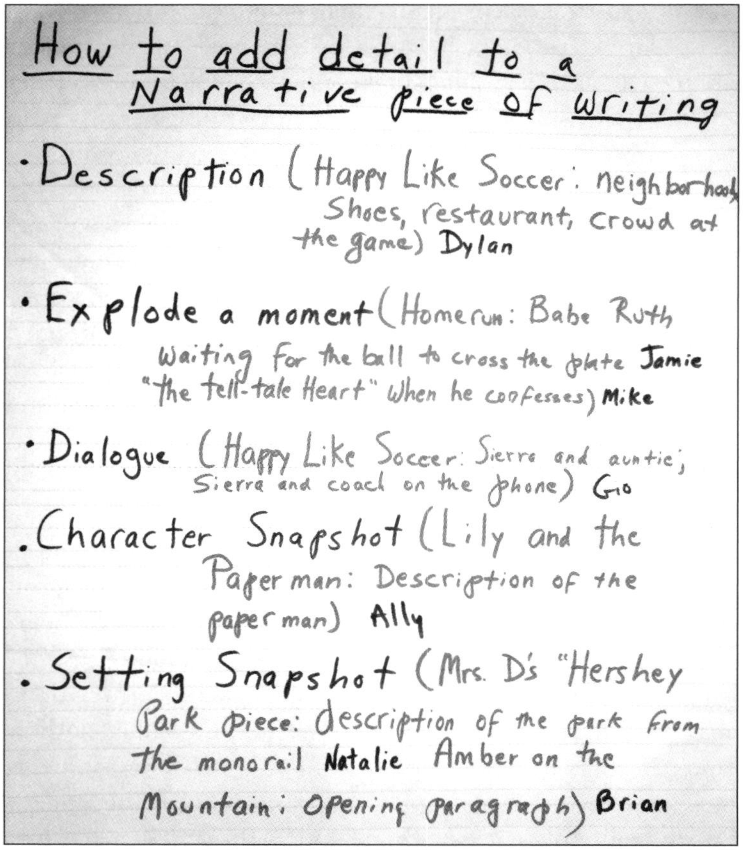

SPOTLIGHT ON FORMATIVE ASSESSMENT

Formative Assessment Using Anchor Charts

Anchor charts are an essential part of any writing classroom. An anchor chart allows teachers to quickly assess students on material that was presented during mini-lessons. Are students applying strategies that were discussed in a mini-lesson? Are students referring to an anchor chart when they write independently? Which anchor chart are they using the most?

Anchor charts are created with the students during mini-lessons. The anchor charts are then posted in the classroom for future reference for both the teacher and the students. It is a great tool for teachers to use to refer to strategies previously taught as a review or as a precursor to future mini-lessons.

Here is an example of an anchor chart I created during our study of nonfiction.

As I observe students, I see them referring to anchor charts during writing workshop. I am also able to refer to strategies when I am conferencing with a student. I can help students recall particular mentor texts and encourage them to try the author's style in their own writing. The quality of writing greatly improves when students are able to visually recall strategies.

Shelly Keller is a kindergarten teacher at the Upper Moreland Primary School. She is on the writing committee and leads writing professional development for the teachers in her school and district. Shelly's students are featured on the pages of this book in several places.

Nonfiction Mentor Texts to Help Us Write

Nonfiction

1. Atlantic by G. Brian Karas

   I am a tree. I have green leaves and apples on me. People like to eat my apples. Squirrels make their home in me. I help people breathe.

2. One Tiny Turtle by Nicola Davies.

   Chameleons are Cool by Martin Jenkins

   Giant Gentle Octopus by Karen Wallace

   Butterflies are colorful.

   Butterflies drink nectar from flowers.

   Butterflies flutter from flower to flower to drink nectar.

3. Supermarket by Kathleen Krull

   The playground is a place you go to play with family and friends. You can find slides, swings, monkey bars, space ship, and round-about. Sometimes there is sand to play with. You can jump rope. You can play hopscotch. Another thing you could do is play basketball or soccer.

4. Sophie Skates by Rachel Isadora

   Surprising Sharks by Nicola Davies

   From Seed to Sunflower by Dr. Gerald Legg

   Diagrams Labels

   Facts at the back of the book

   Seed Sprout Bloom leaf stem petal

   sunflower rose tulip lily

5. Dreamweaver by Jonathan London

   Red-Eyed Tree Frog by Joy Cowley

   My Favorite Bear by Andrea Gabriel

   Bear Facts

   Did You Know?

   Some Facts About Trees

Using Anchor Charts in Kindergarten

Early in the year, Shelly Keller created an anchor chart with the help of her kindergarten students to demonstrate how to add details to a drawing. Shelly's rationale was twofold. First, her students needed to draw pictures because many of them did not yet have the letter-sound correspondence to write words or even to write letters. The detailed drawings would help Shelly understand their scribble writing and attempts to write some letters to represent words. Second, the detailed drawings would help Shelly and her students to read the invented spelling as they progressed throughout the year. Invented, or inventive, spelling is actually highly engineered spelling in which our youngest writers are able to detect phonetic characteristics of words that our English spelling represents. After reading an informational text about frogs, Shelly drew a frog at the top of the anchor chart. "This is like the kind of drawing you might find in a brand-new coloring book," she said.

"Is there anything you can tell me about my frog?" Shelly queried.

Liam responded, "Your frog has big eyes."

Shelly nudged again. "Think about what you would do in your coloring book."

Olivia said, "Frogs are green." Shelly stopped to draw a frog again, this time coloring him green.

"Let's keep adding more details. Where could this frog be found?"

Steven said, "On a lily pad."

Shelly then added a third picture, placing the green frog on a green lily pad. She continued asking questions until the students had placed the frog on a green lily pad in the middle of a blue pond on a sunny day. The pond is surrounded by trees, plenty of rocks to sit on, and two park benches facing the pond. Big orange flowers grow in a field nearby. The students wanted her to add a moon to show that night was falling. In conferences, Shelly often referred to the anchor chart to gently nudge her students to add important details to their drawings, completely filling in the space.

Later in the year, these young writers continued to grow as illustrators. Their detailed drawings helped them with their writing. Shelly modeled with her own story about a roller coaster ride, drawing the pictures first and returning to write her story the next day.

Mia's story (Figure 4.7) is a wonderful example of how a student drew detailed pictures that help readers visualize the scenes. Mia's pictures bring her text to life as she draws the wedding scenes in many colors. Shelly observed Mia several times as she worked through her book's illustrations. Shelly noticed that Mia added details to her pictures. "Can you tell me some of the details you added to this picture, Mia?" pointing to the cover of Mia's book.

"I put red hearts on the dresses to show that the story is about love," Mia replied. "We are smiling because we are so happy. We are holding our baskets. We got to throw petals when we walked to the front of the church."

Figure 4.7
Mia's Wedding Story

"Can you show me another place where you show how people are feeling?" Shelly asked.

Mia turned the pages of her book. "Here. See the people are sitting in the pews. They are all smiling. My Uncle Jamie and Aunt Angel are smiling, too."

"I think this one is my favorite picture, Mia. You placed the guests in pews on each side of the aisle. The flowers, colors, and smiles made me feel the happiness, too."

When the book was published, the class asked Mia some questions about her process as she sat in the author's chair. The kindergarteners asked good questions about how Mia decided on a topic and how she decided what to draw and what to write. Mia had a story in her head about something that really happened. Her connection to writing a beginning, a middle, and an end was not a surprise. Recently, Shelly had spent some time reviewing the organization of a story using two mentor texts, *Night at the Fair* by Donald Crews (an almost wordless book) and *Flora and the Penguin* by Molly Idle, a wordless adventure picture book. Together with the students, they had created a story for each book, writing a beginning, a middle, and an end that matched the pictures. These were anchor charts that the students had used for reference while writing their stories.

Steven: Why did you write about the wedding?

Mia: It was last weekend, and I was a flower girl. I remember everything that happened. It was like a story.

Liam: How did you choose the colors?

Mia: It was like a rainbow. It was so beautiful.

Anna: Who is on the cover?

Mia: The flower girls. Me and my cousin. We have baskets with petals to throw.

Aliana: How did you know what to draw?

Mia: I thought of telling a good story with a beginning, middle, and end.

Liam: How did you know what to write?

Mia: I wrote to match my pictures.

Steven: What is your favorite picture?

Mia: When I drew my Uncle Jamie and Aunt Angel. She had a beautiful dress.

As the school year progressed and kindergartners accompanied their pictures with words and sentences, Shelly decided to talk to them about variation in print. With her students, she constructed an anchor chart using mentor texts, which had been shared as read-alouds with the class previously, to show how authors use variation in print as an interesting feature for their readers.

This print variation includes letter size, varied colors for print, bolded print, unusual placement of letters or words on a page, as well as the style of letters. This anchor chart was constructed over the length of one week. (See Figure 4.8.) For each text, Shelly demonstrated the type of print variation used and had students turn and talk to answer two questions: *Why did the author do this? When could we use it?*

Figure 4.8
Variations in Print

Title and Author	Print Variation	Why did the author do this?	When could we use it?
"Let's Get a Pup!" said Kate by Bob Graham	-names of the dogs are big Dave Rosy	-the names are special and important	-when we want to show an important word
All You Need for a Beach by Alice Schertle	-words are small one tiny grain	-to show the grain is tiny	-to show the size of something
Roller Coaster by Marla Frazee	-different colors -all capitals -word is curved WHOOSH! -words are upside down	-to show which way they are going on the roller coaster	-when we show the direction of the way something is going
Up, Down, Around by Katherine Ayres	-words are curved Pumpkin's vine around and around -words are going down	-to show how things grow	-when something goes down -when something is wavy

Title and Author	Print Variation	Why did the Author do this?	When could we use it?
Mice and Beans by Pam Muñoz Ryan	- Days of the week are a different color Tuesday - a word is a different color snap - a sentence is a different color But it was missing.	-to show the Days of the Week - for the Days of the Week to stand out - to show an important word or sentence	- to show Days of the Week or Months of the Year - to show an important word or sentence
The Way I Feel by Janan Cain	-feelings are different colors "Scared" ANGRY Excited	- to show the feeling	- to show a feeling

Title and Author	Print Variation	Why did the author do this?	When could we use it?
Night Noises by Mem Fox	-big letters -all uppercase letters -letters are a different color -letters bent CLICK	- show onomatopoeia	- when using onomatopoeia
Muncha! Muncha! Muncha! by Candace Fleming	-different color letters -letters bigger Muncha!	-show onomatopoeia	-when using onomatopoeia
Chameleons Are Cool by Martin Jenkins	-big -letters get bigger at the end -letters are thick (bold) thwap!	-show how the chameleon sounds when its tongue gets his food (onomatopoeia)	-when we want to show the sound of something

In *Night Noises* by Mem Fox (1992), Emily noticed that some words were bigger than others. Grace added that in these words all the letters were uppercase. Olivia pointed out that they were written in red and Liam noticed that the letters were a "little curved."

"What was Mem Fox showing us?" Shelly asked. "Turn and talk." After a minute, hands were waving in the air. Nicolas told the class that all the big, red words were sound words. Shelly said, "Yes, sound words are called *onomatopoeia*." Next, Shelly asked them, "Think about your books. When can *you* use this?"

Kegan said, "When you want to say something loud."

Liam added, "When you want to use onomatopoeia." Shelly then asked, "So, how would you do this?"

Jack responded, "Use different colors for the letters."

Grace suggested, "Make them bigger."

Mia asked, "Can we sometimes make them smaller if we want to make them whisper?"

Andrin said, "Make them bigger *and* a different color."

Shelly continued the conversation using the mentor text *Muncha! Muncha! Muncha!* by Candace Fleming (2002). Other mentor texts were demonstrated throughout the week. These rich discussions helped students envision how they would use variation in print in the books they were currently writing.

In another kindergarten classroom, Kolleen Bell had just finished a series of lessons about variation in print and was beginning to talk about adjectives. Kolleen modeled with her own writing, using a beautiful conch shell she displayed for her students. She encouraged them to help her describe her shell with adjectives. The students had many: *smooth on the inside, bumpy on the outside, rough, pink, white, pointy.* She had each student pick a shell from her collection and describe it. Harper started a trend by using variation in print through color and stripes (see Figure 4.9). As Lynne and Kolleen observed the students, they noticed the tracks of Kolleen's teaching in almost all the shell pieces—adjectives were being used and a good many students were making use of the previous focus lessons on variation in print. Even before individual conferences, a trip around the room told Kolleen and Lynne that these kindergarten writers were enjoying trying out the new things they had learned.

Figure 4.9
Harper Writes a Poem About Shells Using Variation in Print

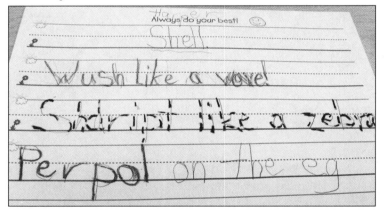

Our Final Thoughts

Anchor charts that are visible in the room are the ones students are currently using. It would not be a good idea to overload environmental print in the classroom with anchor charts posted everywhere. However, these charts are often revisited at other times in a school year. Finding a management system that works is important. In addition, anchor charts can be a messy procedure, and sometimes it's important to redo them so they are neat, organized, and easy to read. It is not necessary to always document the individual thinking with student names or initials, but using this simple strategy some of the time will help students feel important. They are contributing to the writing community and growing as writers.

Chapter 5

ROVING CONFERENCES

> " In a writing conference, the teacher meets with a student one-to-one to talk with him about his writing and to teach him something he needs to become a better writer. The effectiveness of a writing conference depends on the teacher's ability to assess the writers in her class. "
>
> —Carl Anderson, *Assessing Writers*

Roving conferences occur when the teacher checks in with student writers during writing workshop time. Less formal than a one-on-one conference, the roving conference may provide a quick evaluation of a student writer's progress. The teacher peeks over the shoulder of the student writer, asks a few questions, makes notes, and moves on. We might call this type of conference *clipboard cruising* because we do it on the run. Often, a minute or two, but sometimes a little longer, it is an efficient way to check in with many students in a short amount of time. During these conferences, teachers can do several things: praise and support; offer a teaching point, such as a craft move or an editing suggestion; celebrate successes and keep track of the things that students can do; gauge their progress in trying new things; note their willingness to take risks; and ask students to point to places in their pieces where they feel successful or where they may be struggling.

Roving conferences afford students with timely feedback as they write. As Calkins and Ehrenworth state, "Feedback is most potent when students don't yet have mastery and when it is given just in time to learners in the midst of work" (2016, 9). We circulate among our student writers, we observe their writerly behaviors, and we check in with them as they compose, offering support as writers to writers.

Record observations in a fashion that is easy and comfortable for you. (See Appendix 1.) We like to use sticky notes on a clipboard that can be transferred into a binder and onto a page designated for each student. The roving conference gives the teacher precise and brief anecdotal records. Often these notes emphasize the development of ideas and topic choice. The focus is on obstacles the writer may encounter: *So what? Why am I writing this piece? Who is my audience?* Gentle nudges in roving conferences (only a suggestion or two) are often enough to keep the writer engaged and focused. Of course, helping students to link to the learning in the mini-lesson or to the previous day's writing workshop is always beneficial.

Another advantage of roving conferences is that they allow the teacher to touch base with student writers more often, at least once a week. If we rely only on one-on-one conferences, chances are that many weeks will pass before we see each student writer individually.

Early in the school year Diane worked with third-grade students who were writing narratives. Many chose to tell stories about "trick or treat." Essentially, these students are end-of-the-year second graders. Diane peeked over the shoulders of the twenty-one writers as they drafted their pieces. Here are her notes:

> *Many of the writers used minimal details; most were listing. Additionally, twelve writers were using run-together sentences: sentences joined by "and," "and then," "so then." Three of the students (Zen, Colson, and Sarah) have a good sense of sentence. Addison's writing demonstrated not only a good sense of sentence but also used specific details and rich descriptions. Her work can be used as "mentor text" for use of the senses.*
>
> *A secondary need is the use of pronouns (naming oneself last) and use of correct case (me and Alex went trick or treating)—neither Addison nor Sarah appear to make these errors.*
>
> *The above notes were gathered during one writing workshop.*

Prioritizing the information, Kevin Black, the third-grade teacher, and Diane worked on lessons to help the student writers to develop their descriptive details: appeal to the senses and specific word choice (nouns, verbs, and adjectives). Because of the Thanksgiving holiday, Diane, Kevin, and the class brainstormed a list of sights, sounds, tastes, and smells of Thanksgiving (*leaves, football, turkey, pumpkin pie, relatives come to visit, table set for a feast, colder weather, baking smells, roasting smells, cranberry sauce*). Using this list, students brainstormed descriptive words for each (*crunchy fragrant leaves; golden brown turkey; moist, juicy turkey; cinnamon smells; cheers for the Eagles; chattering children; mouthwatering stuffing*). They used their details to write short descriptions about the things they were grateful for at Thanksgiving.

The work on complete sentences and pronoun usage, while postponed for the above lessons, became part of the instruction during mini-lessons and focus lessons in the ensuing weeks in writing workshop. Through roving conferences, Kevin and Diane formed flexible groups for further needed guidance in these areas. As the school year progressed, mini-lessons were selected based on the needs of the students as demonstrated during roving conferences.

The Topic Conference as a Roving Conference

In a topic conference, we help our students to select a topic, narrow that topic, and consider focus and audience. For young writers, these considerations may seem to be monumental tasks. Modeling, thinking aloud as we write, and talking through our choices help students to take these steps themselves. We also confer with students individually in roving conferences to guide them in selecting their topics.

In one fifth-grade classroom, Diane worked with students who were beginning to write informational pieces. In their writer's notebooks, students brainstormed lists of things that they already knew a lot about and that they were curious enough about to want to know more. Trish Ast, their teacher, emphasized that the purpose of this piece was to provide information—to teach. Their audience would be their classmates; they would publish a book of their pieces.

Diane and Trish circulated around the room, looking at the work of the student writers, asking questions, prodding the students in their thinking about their chosen topic. Aubrey's topic was about field hockey. Diane asked, "What do you want the reader to learn about field hockey?" As Aubrey talked about what she knew, Diane noticed that Aubrey's main interest was college field hockey, specifically the availability of hockey scholarships for student athletes. Aubrey plays field hockey and is thinking of her future as a possible college athlete. But what is her topic? Diane asked Aubrey to explain the positions available on a field hockey team. What skills are required for each position? How would an athlete choose a position based on her skills? Which positions offer more opportunities for a player to show off her skills (what would a recruiter see)? As Aubrey and Diane talked about the general topic of field hockey, Aubrey discovered that she could narrow the topic to "four field hockey positions and the skills needed for each." After a few minutes of chatting, Aubrey was ready to go. She had a focus, knowledge about the topic, and questions to research.

Dylan likes to cook. He is interested in spicy foods, and he has a garden where he grows vegetables in the summer. His topic was hot peppers. Diane asked, "Will this be about growing hot peppers or using hot peppers in cooking?" He wasn't sure. Dylan talked about the types of hot peppers and their hotness on the Scoville Heat Scale. Dylan knows a lot about hot peppers. He wondered what gives peppers their heat. Dylan thought that he might write about how to use hot peppers in cooking, using information about three different kinds of peppers easily grown in southeastern Pennsylvania. Diane reminded Dylan of his audience, suggesting that he find a way to make this information interesting to his classmates. He thought that they would like hearing about the Scoville scale. Dylan was ready to begin his piece, too.

Many students selected topics about endangered species: sea turtles and pollinators were two topics shared by several students. The problem with these topics is that student writers rarely know that much about them. Are the writers selecting these topics because they hear so much about endangered species in school? Are they selecting these topics because they believe they can find information without too much effort? Are they truly interested in the issue? Asking these questions in conferences will help us to help our student writers choose and narrow their topics to a subject matter that interests them and is doable.

For some writers, topic conferences may be necessary on most pieces they write. Guiding these writers to focus their ideas to make a point about their topics can help them to get started, so that they're not paralyzed by indecision or overwhelmed by the sheer weight of a subject. Other writers as the year progresses may not need topic conferences. Still others may need a topic conference for one genre of writing but not for another. Roving conferences, in which the teacher peeks over the shoulders of student writers as they plan and compose, are a good vehicle for determining what students need and when they need it.

SPOTLIGHT ON FORMATIVE ASSESSMENT

A Memorable Conference

Through the years, I've conferred with many English language learners, or ELLs. The most memorable conference with an ELL student happened over a decade ago, but I still remember our conference vividly.

Juan and Robert were chatting at table six as writing partners during a full-class share when I pulled alongside them. I asked what they were working on as writers. Juan told me Robert was encouraging him to open his story with dialogue since it wasn't too interesting as he wrote it. I asked Juan what he could do to make his story more interesting so his reader would be hooked from the start. He said, "I can start with dialogue, like Robert suggested, but there's a problem."

"What was the problem?"

"My mom said something to me in Spanish," Juan replied.

"So start your intro paragraph in Spanish," I responded matter-of-factly.

Juan looked shocked. "I can do that?"

"Of course you can," I replied.

Before launching into my teaching point, I took the time to compliment the boys on working well together as writing partners: one for giving specific feedback and the other for taking constructive critcism well. Then, I taught into what Juan was doing by showing him how to code-switch by studying a mentor text. After studying "Josie's First Allowance Day" by Rosie Perez, Juan noticed the text switched between English and Spanish. Therefore, he used the same format as Perez did, by writing the actual Spanish words his mother had said and then translated them so non–Spanish speakers (like me) could understand what he wrote.

Just as I was getting to the end of the conference, Juan lifted his head and asked, "Can I do this on more than one piece?"

I looked right into his big, brown eyes and said, "You bet! Today, and every day you're writing personal narratives, it's smart to remember you can continue to open your stories with dialogue. However, I also want you to remember you can draw on the work done by other authors to help inspire you to write in more creative ways, such as switching between English and Spanish."

Once I gave Juan "permission" to code-switch, he did it regularly in his writing the rest of the year. Not only did this help him write more authentically, but it honored his first language.

As a result of my conference with Juan, I became obsessed with code-switching. I was—and still am—on the lookout for short stories or picture books in which authors weave in a language other than English. I do this as a way to honor ELL students' voices so they have a variety of possibilities for the ways they can code-switch in their own writing.

This conference was an aha moment for me as well. By listening to Juan, who told me he was having a problem, I was able to teach him a skill he will carry with him for the rest of his life. If we can pick up on students' fears when we confer with them, then we can help young children uncover their true selves when they are writing.

Stacey Shubitz is an author, an independent literacy consultant, and an adjunct professor. Her most recent book is *Craft Moves: Lesson Sets for Teaching Writing with Mentor Texts* (Portland, ME: Stenhouse, 2016).

How Roving Conferences Inform Instruction

In a sixth-grade classroom where students were composing argument papers, Diane circulated among the writers as they formulated their thesis statements. Through direct instruction, modeling, and shared practice, students observed and constructed several thesis statements, recognizing (or so the instructors thought) the requisites of a thesis statement for argument writing:

Opinion (debatable claim) + Supportive Facts = Thesis

Through clipboard cruising, Diane discovered that Joey, Jamir, Jamie, Hannah, and Amanda all wrote thesis statements that contained only their opinion without the addition of facts to support that opinion. This observation demonstrated to Diane and Kris Endy, their teacher, the need for small-group reteaching. While students were conducting research on the library computers, Diane took time in the library classroom to guide these five students in formulating their thesis statements to plan their argumentative pieces. When the student writers returned to the classroom the next day, thesis statements were shared on the whiteboard for the whole class to evaluate and discuss. This was time well spent, because the success of a good argument relies on the formulation of a good thesis. Other students, who may have been experiencing similar difficulties, had the opportunity to share their thesis statements as well.

Other clipboard cruising observations during one particular class meeting look like this:

Michael—cut and paste note taking! Reminder chat about plagiarism! Check with class about this.

Natalie—evaluating debate site on *Time for Kids* for reliability (checked dates and names)

Kayla—source takes opposite view. Good for counterargument.

Lily—a similar "aha" moment

Adrianna—changed topic; check on her again tomorrow

Dylan—topic too broad; changed to concussion from football injuries

Notes such as these inform our instruction. We need to know which of our writers are experiencing difficulties with finding information, and we need to be aware of those who are switching topics. Who is taking shortcuts in note taking that can lead to plagiarism? Which students have written sound thesis statements? Which students show that they can evaluate Internet sites? Which student writers can serve as guides to their fellow writers? When the teacher is the only one offering guidance, student writers have just one conferrer. When other students in the class demonstrate that they are experts at a skill, a student writer has more options for guidance and conferences. The writing workshop truly becomes a writing community when the teacher is not the only "expert" in the room.

In the spring, sixth-grade students were writing informational pieces. At this point in the school year, student writers are accustomed to both roving conferences and one-on-one conferences. They have participated in peer conferences, too. In roving conferences during their drafting and revising, Diane and Kris asked students to share something from their drafts that they were proud of writing, as well as something they wanted advice about. Kris and Diane used the students' preparation for the conference as a teachable moment. For example, choosing a section to share that the writer is proud of writing assumes that the student writer has written a multiparagraph draft. If the writer has only a few sentences, chances are there won't be much from which to select. To ask for advice, the writer needs to have thought about the purpose of this piece of writing, as well as how that piece fulfills its purpose. These kinds of conversations, in addition to modeling how to ask for advice, are essential to the success of roving conferences and writing conferences. Writers need to think about what they are putting on the page. Their teachers make decisions about what writers in their classrooms need by observing the writers closely and listening to their questions and responses.

In a conference with Ben, Diane wanted to be sure that he was using his own words (paraphrasing), not copying word for word the information he acquired through research. Ben's piece is about the invention of Braille, and, though Ben did have experience and knowledge of the topic, he added details and specific information from published sources. Diane asked Ben to show her where he used information from another source. Diane was pleased to discover that Ben did paraphrase in an expert fashion; he could be a resource for students who are having difficulty paraphrasing. His strategy was to write what he remembered without looking back at the page he read. This strategy precludes Ben from copying, because he is writing from memory and is not tempted to use the original author's words instead of his own. After completing the paraphrase, he checked back with the source again to be sure his information was accurate. This one-book-open-at-a-time strategy is one that can be readily imitated by his classmates. In addition, Diane also noticed that Ben began his piece by involving the reader in a *what if* scenario and asking a question. Diane pointed out why that was a successful opening: "It made me wonder what I would do in that situation." Be specific with a student about why a craft use is successful. Students are more inclined to repeat successes when they know how their writing affects readers.

Kayla's conference focused on her organizational format: compare and contrast. Kayla's piece is about two types of competitive cheerleading. To help her organize the piece, she used a Venn diagram (something other students might find convenient). The information on the diagram helped her to develop paragraphs that explain each kind of cheerleading—what they had in common and how they were different. Her draft jumps right in with a description of the similarities and differences between the two types of cheerleading.

Diane Confers with Kayla, Grade Six
http://sten.pub/ac01

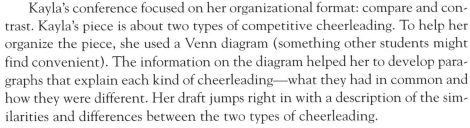

The similarities and differences between something can be large. You may not think that there would be two types of cheerleading, but there is. The two types of cheerleading are recreational cheerleading and all-star cheerleading. It may seem that there probably is nothing different between the two, but there is.

In a previous quick check, Diane reminded Kayla of the lead mini-lessons, encouraging her to go back to her writer's notebook to discover how she had practiced using them. The next day, during a roving conference, Diane noticed that Kayla had revised her opening paragraph to catch the reader's attention, as well as to set the purpose for reading.

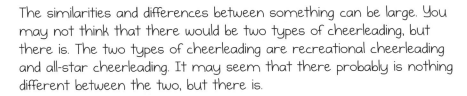

The loud music is blaring with the sound of remixed tunes. The aroma of junk food fills your nostrils. A stage takes up most of the space on the floor of the convention center. You look towards the stage and see a group of girls. They have high hair and glittered uniforms. This is an all-star team. Then you notice another group of girls, all with different hair styles and plain uniforms with the school name stitched across the front. This is a recreational cheerleading squad. Besides looking different, the teams perform differently too. They are different in style, purpose, and time limitations.

Kayla used a set-the-scene opening, bringing the reader into the audience at a competition by describing what audience members would experience as the participants get ready to compete. Her last sentences tell the reader what to expect to learn by reading her piece. She also sets up the structure of the piece as compare and contrast. To move Kayla forward, Diane asked her to talk through how she will organize the piece in the remaining paragraphs. Compare and contrast can be a difficult organizational strategy to master. Helping Kayla by having her talk through her planning made it less daunting and more doable. Because this conference was a quick-check roving conference, Diane made a note of where Kayla was in the process and moved on. Had Kayla's graphic organizer been lacking or had she been unable to articulate her plans for organizing the piece, Diane would have continued with the conference. Roving conferences not only give teachers the opportunity to check in with student writers but also have the advantage of pinpointing precisely what student writers need and when they need it.

Sometimes students have questions about their endings. A quick-check with Lily reveals that she doesn't like her ending because, she says, it sounds repetitive. Diane questioned Lily's intent: *What do you want to leave the reader with? What is your big idea? What point does your thesis statement make? How can that point be restated?*

Here is the opening of Lily's draft:

> Imagine sitting on a stage playing a violin. The elegant sound of the strings vibrating. Hearing the applause from the audience after your favorite song. Wouldn't that be amazing? The violin is a fun and amazing-sounding instrument, but how does one play? What is the violin made of and how is the sound made?

Here is the draft ending:

> The violin is a fun and amazing-sounding instrument that is easy to play and is made of wood and metal. It's a pleasure to play the violin.

Because Lily's stumbling block right now is organizing, specifically, her ending, Diane addressed that issue. Let the student control the conference. Through questioning Lily's intent, Diane guided Lily not only to think about possible ways to end the piece but also to use specific details. Lily suggests that

Diane Confers with Lily, Grade Six
http://sten.pub/ac02

it's important to know the aspects of the violin's structure, as well as how to play it. Diane asks, *Why?* Getting Lily to think about why her information is important to a reader, Diane steers Lily toward making decisions about possible ways to end the piece. As teachers and writing coaches, we do not make decisions for our writers. Though we can suggest possibilities, the final decisions for any writing piece come from the writer.

Here is Lily's revised ending:

> The violin takes you to your imagination. When someone plays the violin they get taken away to a place where no thoughts interrupt. When you play the violin you leave the real world for a moment in time and retreat to your imagination.

Sometimes gentle nudges are enough to move writers forward; sometimes more direct instruction or reminders of previous lessons may be required.

Roving conferences also give teachers the opportunity to encourage student writers to think back to mini-lessons and to use the strategies taught in them. When Michael needed to define terms, Diane reminded him that definitions are a way to add content to a piece of informational writing. In Michael's case his topic "flowboarding" is something he knows a great deal about, but it's not something about which most readers would have knowledge.

> Flowboarding is a fun sport for doing awesome tricks. In flowboarding, I practice by taking off my trucks from my skateboard and I do carpet boarding. It is good because it's fun, and I get a good practice from it. If I can land the trick more than one time, I would try it on the flowrider machine. Flowboarding is fun to land fun and great tricks.

Diane asked Michael a series of questions: *What are "trucks"? What is "carpet boarding"? Why is it "good practice"? Can you describe one of the tricks you would try to master? What's a "flowrider machine"?* Diane reminded Michael of the mentor texts the class had studied. When an unfamiliar term is introduced for the first time, an author defines the term. Most readers of Michael's piece would not know the answers to the questions Diane asked Michael. Helping Michael to see the need for definition gave him a way to add content to his piece in addition to making his meaning clear.

Students have an important role in the roving conference. Preparing students to participate in a roving conference is time well spent. Because roving conferences are quick exchanges, students need to be prepared to discuss their writing. For the conferences in sixth grade, Diane asked students to show what they thought they did well and to share a place in their writing where they might need advice or feedback. The important factor is that students accept responsibility for preparing for the conference. Provide one or two sentence starters or questions to get student writers ready. For example, *I'm writing*

Diane Confers with Michael, Grade Six
http://sten.pub/ac03

about . . . I need help with . . . I want my reader to know . . . My focus is . . . I'm working on this skill . . . . Writers are thinkers. They come to the conference having already reflected on what they have written, where they have had success, what they are trying out, and what specifically they need feedback on. For primary grade writers, an anchor chart prominently displayed in the classroom can be used as a guide:

I am writing about . . .

My favorite part is . . .

One thing I wonder about . . .

Our Final Thoughts

The teacher's job in a roving conference involves reacting to the text specifically, particularly the part that the student writer has pointed out. The teacher may also use the roving conference to teach a quick lesson (define terms, for example), remind the writer of a craft lesson already taught, or to provide a resource (mentor text or anchor chart). In a roving conference, teachers do not edit but nudge writers forward, spending brief spurts of time connecting with student writers in the workshop setting.

Chapter 6

TEACHER AND STUDENT
One-on-One, Small-Group, and Whole-Group Conferences

" My collaborations with kids take many forms. I ask leading
questions, suggest options a writer might pursue, intervene
when a writer moves off-track, point a new direction,
demonstrate solutions to writing problems, show how to
achieve an effect, even make brief assignments that invite
students to engage as writers in ways they otherwise might
not. My role as responder is more diverse these days, and
more satisfying. I am teaching, and my students are producing
writing they like, can learn from, and take pride in. "

—Nancie Atwell, *In the Middle: New Understandings About Writing,
Reading, and Learning*

The One-on-One Student-Teacher Conference

Student-teacher conferences are at heart of the writing workshop. Although we
can't always get to everyone in a day, we can try to see each individual student
in a week's time, sometimes spilling over into the next week. During workshop,
many kinds of conferences will be employed. You will most likely use roving
conferences daily and often hold whole-group conferences as opportunities for
final reflection to close each workshop. One-on-one conferences are most effective if you have an established routine and keep it short—three to five minutes
as often as possible. A simple routine might include getting the big picture, that
is, understanding what the student is trying to accomplish (his point or purpose
for writing) using the tracks of your teaching (the strategies or craft moves).
Make a note of those craft moves, mechanics skills, and organizational strategies the student does fairly well. Ask him one or two questions if he needs to fill

in some important details, developing his ideas through descriptions, explanations, examples, anecdotes, quotes from the experts, and statistics, depending on the type of writing, purpose, and audience. Then provide a gentle nudge. Decide what this student is able to try to improve her piece, and more importantly, to grow as a writer. Here, you might think about the standards as well as the zone of proximal development. According to Lev Vygotsky, "What the child can do in cooperation today he can do alone tomorrow" (1989, 189). Frank Smith (1988) calls this interaction a social and collaborative basis for learning. Whatever you call it, the mentoring relationship in a teacher-student conference helps to make writing situations more like writing in the real world. Writing is not a solitary but a collaborative act. Mentors include the books we read, our favorite authors, and our peers. In the real world, writers have conversations with their editors, and in the classroom, writers have conversations with their teachers. During the conference, place this particular work the student has brought to you within the larger context of the ongoing work of the writing workshop.

If you are writing in your writer's notebook and modeling for your students, you will have practice solving writing problems that occur in the context of your own writing. The practice of writing in your own writer's notebook will make you a better conference partner, as you will confer as writer to writer instead of teacher to student writer. After using a conference routine for several months, you'll become an expert, and conferences will become second nature. In the beginning, a reminder list is helpful. As Lucy Calkins has often told us, we should think about teaching the writer instead of focusing on the piece of writing. We need to listen carefully to what a student tells us in a conference, trying to understand the student's needs in order to know what direction the conference will take. Lynne asks her students to bring their writer's notebooks with them to a conference if the draft they are sharing is written somewhere else. The notebook gives her the big picture and helps her decide what one thing might move a writer forward, improving the future writing pieces he will create.

Questions for Conferring Around the Types of Writing

One-on-one conferences are more efficient if you are ready with some key questions to advance the writer and the writing. For older students, such as fourth-grade through middle school writers, it is even a good idea to give them a copy of questions for each writing type. That way, they can be ready to respond to you and possibly clean up some fuzziness or confusion before you see them. We are not saying that you have to ask all these questions or even that you have to use any of them. We do think that brainstorming essential conference questions for each writing type will help you to prepare to move through four or more one-on-one conferences each day. That way, it will be possible to keep conferences to three to five minutes and see everyone at least once in any given week. Laminate your pages of questions and keep them in a folder or binder on your desk or another key location for easy access. Add to your list, depending on your class's individual strengths and needs. Natural abilities and skill development vary from year to year, even in the same grade level!

Questions for Narrative Writing
- Is your story about one thing?
- Are you telling the inside story (the one nobody knows but you) or the outside story?
- How did you introduce the setting?
- What do you need to do next?
- Is there a place for a splash of dialogue?
- What is the problem in your story?
- How do you reveal your characters to your readers?

Questions for Informational Writing
- What is your text about? What made you choose this topic?
- Did you present the information in a logical order?
- What sources did you use?
- How did you take notes?
- Why would anybody want to know this information?
- How did you develop your ideas? Anecdotes? Statistics? Quotes from experts? Facts? Opinions? Descriptions?

Questions for Opinion/Argument Writing
- What made you choose this topic and position?
- Show me where you state your opinion clearly.
- What is your most important evidence to support your opinion?
- What sources did you use? How did you include them in this piece?
- What kind of tone (expert? angry? whiny?) does your piece have? What makes you think so?

With your colleagues, take a moment to reflect on why we hold writing conferences with our students. When conferring with your students, what are the overall goals you hope to accomplish? When you think about these goals, do they change based on the mode of writing you are teaching? Why or why not? Think about the types of writing and mentor authors you study when you create essential conference questions for each of these types or author study. (See Appendixes 2–5.)

Purposes for Conferring

There are many kinds of conferences. The topic conference can be useful if your students need help in finding out what they want to write about or narrowing or broadening a topic. Teachers discover how students can independently handle choosing a topic that they can wrap their arms around. In Chapter 5, "Roving Conferences," you are invited to peek over the shoulders of several students who are deciding on topics for an informational piece. For many young writers in the beginning of the year, a topic conference may be necessary each time they begin a new genre. Knowing your writers and their needs is what makes for a successful writing workshop. On any given day, you may decide to hold only one kind of conference, or you may find yourself holding several different types of conferences. We hope these bulleted points can guide your thinking.

Topic Search Conference
- To help students generate a list of possible topics.
- To help to narrow the topic.
- To find a focus or a *so what*.
- Teacher can be the recorder and hand over list at the end of conference.
- Sometimes in pairs or in small groups to generate more good ideas.

Process Conferences
- What are you working on?
- How is it coming?
- What are you going to do next?
- Goal: to help person become more reflective and self-reliant.

Status of the Class
- Whole-group conference at beginning of workshop.
- Each student makes a public commitment to some kind of work.
- Students may run status of the class and record in upper grades.

Content Conference
- Conversations aimed at discussing and developing ideas.
- To develop the meaning or content inside a research report.
- Teacher may offer information, authors, and sources.

Ear Conference
- Read aloud the entire piece or a portion.
- A way to hear own work and get a sense of flow.
- Students can be encouraged to pause as they notice problems or get new ideas.
- Teacher can read a section to the student, pausing to allow students to make changes or to note problem areas.

Evaluation Conference
- Stress ongoing process of inquiry and search for revisions.
- Outcomes—specific writing goals entered in a log or folder.
- A form—portfolio conference scheduled quarterly.
- Sometimes can involve the student in the grading process or ask for a written self-evaluation as a product of the conference.

Notice/Ponder/Polish
- Often a small-group or whole-group conference.
- Look for writer's strengths to praise. Be specific.
- Are you left with any questions as the reader?
- Offer one key suggestion for improvement.

Eye Conference
- Focus here is on editing.
- Sit side by side; reviewer has control of the text.
- Look at editing items one at a time: capitalization, paragraphing, punctuation, spelling.
- Student writer can be encouraged to take a risk with punctuation—trying something new, such as a dash, a colon, parentheses, quotation marks, or ellipses.

Because eye conferences are editing conferences, they are reserved for those pieces that will be published and will not occur on every piece a student writes. We suggest that eye conferences occur only between student and teacher. They should not become peer conferences. Peers will sometimes correct errors that don't exist, skip over actual errors, or focus on perceived errors rather than content. According to Overmeyer (2015, 86), "The biggest danger in allowing peers to provide advice on conventions is that students will tend to take their friend's advice, even if it is wrong."

Conference Goals

The goal of a one-on-one writing conference is not to fix a piece of writing for the writer. The conference is not about just one piece of writing; the conference is about the writer and how to move the writer forward. As Carl Anderson writes: "[M]y role in a conference is to find out *from* students what work they are doing as writers and then teach them how to do that work better" (2000, 25). What does the writer need? What strategy or strategies can be demonstrated to writers in a conference that they will be able to use not only in the piece they are writing today but also in future pieces? We like to start our conferences with an open-ended question: for example, *What can I help you with today?* or *What are you most proud of writing today?* We listen to the student writer, and we read and react to the text. We use the conference as a teaching moment, reminding the writer of an already taught craft lesson or providing a quick review lesson. We make time for the student writer to try it out and to talk through how she might use this strategy again in other pieces of writing. We use the student writing to teach the writer, to decide what the writer needs and what teaching will help this writer, not only in this piece of writing.

In *The One-on-One Reading & Writing Conference*, Berne and Degener discuss "stretch comments": comments that are "appropriately challenging and developmentally in sync with student needs" (2015, 62). Keep in mind that as conferrers our goal is to challenge student writers. Challenge them to write better today than they did yesterday and to take risks, try things out, make decisions about crafting more effective writing. All of this is what makes writing workshop active and alive.

Students Need to Be Part of the Process

Of course, one way to challenge our students is to make sure we involve them in the process. When we have a one-on-one or small-group conference, we want students to ask questions and to come up with their own solutions for the problems they may have with their writing. At the very least, they must be part of the conversation about the writing topic, mentor texts, and strategy choice. Students must learn how they can come to a conference prepared to join in rather than to expect that the teacher will just tell them what they should do. In *Writing Workshop: The Essential Guide*, Ralph Fletcher and Joann Portalupi (2001) suggest that we read the student's writing to him so that he can start the conference by reacting to his own words. They urge teachers to let their students lead the way, sometimes by asking for help with a problem they are having difficulty solving on their own. Ultimately, teachers can offer suggestions, but it is up to the writer whether to use a suggestion to revise. Fletcher and Portalupi remind teachers to be positive and to give their students the time in a conference to explain what they are doing and why it is important. They advise us that "you'll need a generous heart, a long-range perspective, plenty of tact, patience, and stamina. A sense of humor doesn't hurt, either" (2001, 59). The chart in Figure 6.1 displays what Lynne and Diane use as guidelines for teacher and student during a one-on-one conference.

In the Primary Classroom: Student-Teacher Conferences in Action

In Kolleen Bell's kindergarten, the students were excited to try out variation in print in their writing pieces. Kolleen had shared *Don't Let the Pigeon Drive the Bus!* and *The Pigeon Needs a Bath!* by Mo Willems. Two of the students' favorites were *The Way I Feel* by Janan Cain and *My Mouth Is a Volcano!* by

The Role of the Teacher	The Role of the Students
Demonstrate setting a purpose for the conference.	Make a list of what worked for you and questions you may have.
Listen to the student read all or part of the piece of writing.	Set a purpose for active listening before starting to read.
Question the writer to help him move forward. (It's about the writer, not the writing!)	Be specific in your response. Find evidence in your text.
Actively listen.	Actively listen.
Take notes on an index card or sticky notes. Make the students (primary grades) a copy of your suggestion (a nudge).	For older students, take a few notes. Record a polish. For younger students, tell your teachers what you heard and will do next.
Teach if it is important.	Ask questions for anything you do not understand. Try out the suggestions somewhere.
Create a writing goal.	Be active in the goal-setting process.

Figure 6.1
Roles for One-on-One
Conferences

Julia Cook, two picture books in which the print is often written in an unconventional manner to match the thoughts and feelings the words convey. Lynne conferred with James, who wrote a piece about rocks after examining a display at his table. He took a great deal of time to write down some thoughts using this new strategy. Lynne praised James, referenced the mentor texts, and asked him to explain his thinking. She hinted at a suggestion: not all the words needed to be changed into artwork because it could make the piece too hard to read and take too long to finish. She opened a pathway for thinking about this, but she did not tell James exactly what to do the next time. Lynne kept the focus of this conference on James's use of variation in print. He was trying something new for the first time, taking a risk. To keep conferences under five minutes, it is best to choose a focus for discussion and a polish. Keep in mind that too many suggestions are confusing to a young writer. Besides, writing cannot be taught in one conference. Each conference will provide a new layer of meaning and skill.

Lynne: James, the letters look so fancy! They look like a piece of art!

James: Yes. I played with the words.

Lynne: What do you mean?

James: That's what Ms. Bell calls it. We looked at books where the letters were different sizes and colors and shapes. Not the regular way you see words in books.

Lynne: Can you explain your piece to me and why you used it here?

James: Sure. Rocks are bumpy and have different shapes. I wanted to make my words look like rocks. And I used a red crayon to go over the word *red* and an orange crayon for *orange*.

Lynne: You really helped me "feel" what rocks are like to touch, even though I didn't have any in my hands.

James: (*nodding*) That's why I did it.

Lynne: So you did what Julia Cook did in *My Mouth Is a Volcano!* by making your words into artwork. Using different colors is a great way to change up your print, too. What did Candace Fleming do in *Muncha! Muncha! Muncha!*? What do you notice in this book? (*Lynne hands the book to James.*)

James: Different sizes and some letters are capitalized that shouldn't be. (*He points to the title page.*)

Lynne: Are all the words written that way?

James: No.

Lynne: Why not, do you think?

James: That would take a lot of time!

Lynne: Yes. And maybe it would make the book too hard to read.

James: (*nodding his head*) It would be hard.

Lynne also had a conference with Jordyn who wanted to use variation in print to write about bees (see Figure 6.2). "I can hear the bees, Jordyn!" Lynne told her as Jordyn showed her work. Lynne praised her for the fancy letter formation and the use of capital letters. She asked Jordyn about the additional letters in the word *buzz* the second time she wrote it. Jordyn shared, "I wanted the readers to say this really loud and for a long time." Lynne nodded. "Oh, you wanted the reader to stretch out the word when saying it out loud. That makes

Figure 6.2
Jordyn Uses Variation in Print to Write About Spring

good sense. Let's read your piece together and try it out." When they read Jordyn's piece, other young writers wanted to join them and read it again. Jordyn was pleased that her classmates enjoyed her piece, too. When you share writing, it is always a celebration. Lynne saw students in Kolleen's class trying out new things and having fun at the same time. The kindergarteners believed they were writers and could write just like the published authors they were reading. Remember that learning can be both challenging and joyful.

On a sunny March morning, Grayson asked Kolleen for a conference. He was eager to share his piece about dinosaurs and was very proud of his drawing. He knew, too, that he was going to be videotaped for Lynne's book. Kolleen began by asking Grayson to state his goal. He found it on the goal chart in the conference center: "I will add more sentences." When Kolleen asked him to count his sentences, he counted four when he originally had two. As Kolleen questioned Grayson about adding more details about dinosaurs, Grayson told her they had big teeth. Although Kolleen helped him with the word *sharp*, she encouraged him to spell it on a sticky note. Grayson had time to add the sentence to his journal entry and revised his drawing to make the teeth look even sharper. (See Figure 6.3a.)

Later that afternoon, Kolleen showed Lynne several pieces Grayson had written two months before the conference on the dinosaur piece (Figure 6.3b).

Grayson Confers with Ms. Bell
on a Writing Goal
http://sten.pub/ac04

Figure 6.3a
Grayson Adds a Sentence to His Dinosaur Piece

Figure 6.3b
Grayson Uses a Detailed Drawing with One Sentence (*Presents make me happy.*)

Looking at the two pieces, Lynne could immediately notice the change in confidence and the increased commitment to writing thoughts down on paper. When Grayson entered kindergarten, he couldn't write his name. By March, he was trying to spell difficult words on his own, using end punctuation, and trying out variation in print (*I like roaring [rrrooogg] dinosaurs!*). In the future, Kolleen said she would like to get Grayson to be more consistent with spacing and the use of uppercase letters. She hoped that she could hold some group conferences for a few kindergarteners about adding a final s to a plural noun and perhaps think about beginning their sentences in different ways.

Kolleen shared her method for record keeping for her one-on-one conferences. She uses the inside pages of a manila folder, placing square boxes in rows and listing the students' names in alphabetical order. Then she applies different-colored sticky notes to indicate where they are in the writing process, as well as what they talked about during their conferences. "This helps me keep track of the writers' progress and gives me opportunities for flexible grouping. The system is easy to manage and works for me." Lynne agreed. It is important to maintain a record-keeping system that is not so complex that you don't want to use it regularly. (See Figure 6.4.)

In Shelly Keller's kindergarten class, large 5-by-8-inch index cards are placed in manila folders with a student's name written at the bottom of each card. Shelly has sets based on tables where the students are seated. In this way, she can use one set to circulate around a table, or sometimes two, more efficiently during workshop time. Shelly jots notes about what students are trying

Figure 6.4
Record Keeping for One-on-One Conferences

Figure 6.5
Record Keeping in Shelly Keller's
Kindergarten Class

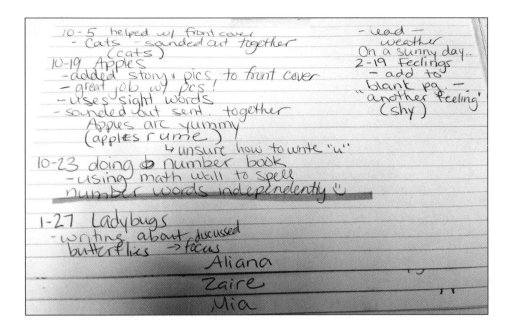

out and what they talked about in the conference. Often, she tries to note whether students are creating detailed drawings, adding labels or speech bubbles, and something about their attempts with kid spelling and use of sight words. In addition, Shelly is looking for evidence of the tracks of her teaching. On Aliana's card she noted the use of a weather lead and a discussion about focus. (See Figure 6.5.)

SPOTLIGHT ON FORMATIVE ASSESSMENT

Formative Assessment While Conferring with a First Grader

Hunter, a first grader, came to the table for a conference carrying a large volume of collected stories by Dr. Seuss in addition to his writing. Earlier, his teacher had asked the class to review what they were currently working on. If they needed help with something they were to jot it on a sticky note before their conference. Hunter was in the process of writing a nonfiction piece about Dr. Seuss, and his sticky note indicated he wanted help with "bold beginnings" and "interesting facts." Right away, I understood that this was a young writer who knew something about informational writing and perhaps his needs as a writer. At this young age, he was beginning to form a writing identity.

As Hunter explained what he was doing, I realized that he was confusing the reference information at the end of the book for a listing of facts. After explaining to him that what he was looking at was information that told where and when each story was made, Hunter looked disappointed. Clearly, these were not the interesting facts he was looking for. Luckily, I had noticed that some of the references were photo credits, so I flipped to the front pages and discovered that the collection opened with biographical information on Dr. Seuss, complete with pictures.

"Hunter, I think I can show you how to find some interesting facts about Dr. Seuss. Would you like me to show you?" I asked.

"Sure," he replied.

I pointed to a picture of Ted Geisel as a young man with two small children. We talked about the picture, and I explained that one of his facts might be that Dr. Seuss had two children, a boy and a girl. Then we looked at a picture of the author as a young boy proudly holding a fish on a rod.

"What can you tell me about this picture?" I asked.

"I think he liked to go fishing," said Hunter. "And look at this one. I think he was in the Army! And I could say that his real name was Ted."

"How did you know that?" I questioned.

"I can read some of those words," Hunter replied, pointing to a caption.

The quick formative assessment during this conference told me that while Hunter had some knowledge about informational writing, he needed to learn more ways to discover facts that were within his grasp. Showing him how to get information from pictures and his own discovery about the use of captions quickly became part of his schema for gathering information. Later, Hunter was asked to share his process with the class, and the strategies became part of whole-group learning.

Rose Cappelli is a literacy consultant and former reading specialist. She is coauthor with Lynne Dorfman of three books with Stenhouse: *Mentor Texts: Teaching Writing Through Children's Literature, K–6, Second Edition* (2017); *Nonfiction Mentor Texts: Teaching Informational Writing Through Children's Literature, K–8* (2009); and *Poetry Mentor Texts: Making Reading and Writing Connections, K–8* (2012).

In Upper Elementary Grades: Student-Teacher Conferences in Action

Let's take a look at Jamie, a sixth-grade student, creating an informational text. Jamie is writing about the care and feeding of a dwarf hamster. Diane begins the conference by asking Jamie what she likes best about what she's written so far. Jamie likes her lead and reads it aloud.

> Imagine this, the care taker is untrained and washes their new Chinese dwarf hamster. They did not do enough research and now their hamster is at the vet sick and hurting. Hospital bills pile up on the desk, there goes the summer vacation that has been planned for months. Make sure to do research before you decide to get a Chinese dwarf hamster. Proper food and care are very important when owning a pet. Also look into cost. This is how to take care of a Chinese dwarf hamster.

Diane tells Jamie what she did well. "You really make the reader understand why it's important to know how to care for the hamster when you provide the description of the ailing animal. You also let the reader know that poor care can result in expensive veterinary bills. So, you give us a purpose for reading." Jamie asks for advice about her ending. She can't think of a good way to sum things up. "Everything that I write sounds repetitive. I'm just saying the same thing in the end that I said in the beginning. What should I do?" This question provides an opportunity to teach a strategy for ending informational pieces. Satisfying endings are difficult to write in a nonnarrative piece. Diane used Jamie's question about her ending to do a quick lesson on endings as a summing up of information. She advised Jamie to answer the question, *So what? Why should the reader care? Why do you (the writer) care? Can the piece suggest a course of action? What should the pet owner do?* Give the reader something to think about. Diane asked Jamie to try it out by talking through these questions. Then, Diane asked Jamie where else Jamie could envision using this *so what* strategy again. What other genres of writing would lend themselves to this kind of ending? After the conference, Diane left Jamie to revise her piece and to add an ending. Jamie is on her way to completing her informational piece about the care of a Chinese dwarf hamster. She has experience with the topic, has ample materials for research, and has decided on an organizational pattern. Conferring with Jamie at the start and allowing her to talk through her piece was the best strategy for moving her forward as a writer. Always allow the student writer to direct the conference, taking cues from the writer's needs and concerns. Conferences are not the time to fix the writing; they are opportunities for feedback.

Izzy, another sixth grader, was having difficulty getting started with her informational piece. In a previous roving conference, Diane and Izzy talked about the how-to format as a way to provide information. "What is something you are good at and can teach someone else to do?" Diane asked. Izzy said she was good at being sneaky! In probing that idea, Diane suggested that the word *sneaky* had negative connotations. People don't like sneaks. Izzy decided that the word *secret* might be a better way to describe what she meant. Diane also asked Izzy to consider the purpose of being secretive. When and why would anyone want to or need to be secretive? Izzy thought about the question and responded, "When you are playing hide and seek." Diane asked Izzy to try an opening (lead) using the hide-and-seek idea to introduce her topic. Later, Izzy connected the ability to be secret to an occupation (store detective). Izzy's lead describes hiding in a closet:

> Hide and seek is a great practice for being sneaky, stealthy, and secret. Once I hid in a closet and blended in with the dresses. People looked in the closet and left without noticing me. Being sneaky, stealthy, and secret is important because you never know what future awaits you.

This draft lead is a good start. Revision will come later, but for now, Izzy has an idea for a how-to piece, as well as a way to connect the instruction to

Izzy Confers with Diane
on Her Lead
http://sten.pub/ac05

future experiences. Izzy, a reluctant writer who felt she had nothing interesting to say, became more confident about writing once she was able to use her own experiences to inform readers about her ability to blend in and be secret.

Think of the one-on-one conference as a chance to discover what your writers know and can do. Celebrate the successes and let the student writer structure the conference. Jamie didn't ask about spelling; she didn't want to talk about commas. She was concerned about structuring her piece. Responding to that concern was the first priority.

Small-Group Conferences

Small-Group Conference
in Second Grade
http://sten.pub/ac06

Small-Group Conference with
Storyboards in Third Grade
http://sten.pub/ac07

Small-group conferences are useful. In second grade, Kelly Gallagher often uses small-group conferences to strengthen her writing community and to give her young writers a chance to listen in as she offers praise, asks questions, and gives a push.

In this conference, Kelly had the chance to ask one second grader to help another. Her suggestion to Ella had been to try showing emotion at the end of her piece instead of telling it. This craft move was something the second graders had been working on for the past two weeks. Kelly had returned to a read-aloud, *Trouper* by Meg Kearney (2013), to demonstrate how the author revealed things about Trouper, a dog with three legs. When Kelly heard Whitney's piece and her show-not-tell simile (*My heart was as cold as snow*), she knew that pairing the two girls would be perfect. Kelly tries to do this whenever it is possible. "Everyone is a writing teacher," Kelly said. Lynne wholeheartedly agreed!

Brenda Krupp held a small-group conference with four third graders who used storyboards to help them plan their narratives. She asked leading questions of all the group members, noting the difference in their storyboards.

Turner talked about the inclusion of a square for the story problem, stating that the first two boxes had been used to introduce the setting and characters. Ryan had some additional words and symbols to help him know whether it was his character's thoughts, emotions, or actions. Mya had used sticky notes to do some revision as early as her plan because she realized that the problem in her story had been solved too easily. Claire talked about her "hints" where she was going to use the strategy of show, not tell and another place where she would include an exploded moment to slow down the pace of her story. Both would make her story more interesting. The students reflected on the use of storyboards. Claire talked about how the plan would be a good reminder while they were writing. The students agreed that they would use a storyboard again. By holding this small-group conference, the students were able to share the different techniques they had used with their storyboards. For Brenda, it was formative assessment—she was learning about how her students handled this new strategy and how they felt about it. She could see that this group of students

Brenda Krupp's Small-Group
Conference with JD and Jax
http://sten.pub/ac08

had found ways to take this particular strategy and make it their own. (See Figures 6.6a and 6.6b.)

In Brenda's third-grade classroom, Jaxson and JD are joined by their teacher for a small-group conference. Jax is asking for something very specific. He wants help with his lead. JD thought maybe Jax should talk about his main character. Brenda asked JD to read his opening paragraph and then asked Jax what he noticed. Jax noted that he introduced his main characters and talked about the problem in the story. Brenda asked for an explanation of the problem. Jax retold what he had heard. Brenda noted that in Jax's piece, it takes a bit of writing before the reader finds out anything about the character. Then she asked what his lead would sound like if he tried a character lead instead of a weather lead. Jax came up with a new lead: *Carter loved basketball, but someone got in his way.* JD agreed, and Brenda noted how this new lead created tension as well.

Figure 6.6a
"Soccer Girl" by Ryan

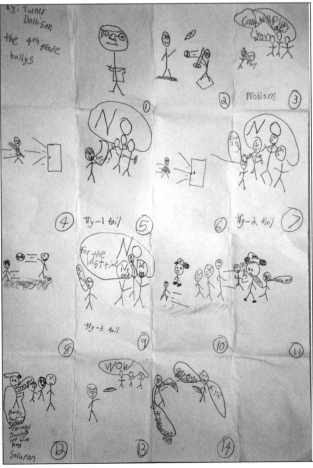

Figure 6.6b
"The Fourth-Grade Bullies" by Turner

Whole-Group Conferences

In March, Kolleen Bell gathered her kindergarten writers on the rug near a chart stand. She was always trying to embed some spelling help as she introduced new genres and new craft moves to her students. In the past several weeks, she had finished several focus lessons on elaboration, variation in print, and end punctuation. She also had revisited lessons on spacing between words and sentences and when to use an uppercase letter. Now she was moving on to a new genre, writing poems.

The students had already used an organizational scaffold, *I'm waiting for . . .* to write one poem. Kolleen felt that attempts at spelling words to approximate the adult spelling had been a little lax, and it was time to give students some more help. She said, "Writers, I was looking at your writing in your journals yesterday and noticed so many of you are taking risks and trying to spell new words. Today, I'm going to try to give you some strategies for spelling sounds in your words. We are going to do some interactive writing, where you and I share the marker, and we'll make a list of spring words for your poems. We'll list them on this anchor chart. Right now, time to talk with a partner and count on your fingers. How many different spring words can you come up with?" The students immediately began to share and count their words. Kolleen called them back: "Let's title our chart *Spring Things* and start to write our words here. How many syllables are in the word *spring*? (The students clapped one syllable.) Do you have your ear ready? In your writing, many of you wrote *s-p-i-n-g* in your poems. What sound is missing? Let's say the word. (They say it chorally three times.) What sound is missing here (Kolleen points to *sp—ing* on the chart)?"

"RRRRRRRRRRRR!"

"That's right!"

Kolleen reviewed how to use the lines on the chart paper to print. "Do your finest handwriting on this chart when you come up to help me. Let's stretch out the sounds you hear in each word we put on our list." Amiyah volunteered *sun*.

"How many sounds do you hear in *sun*?" The students put up three fingers after Kolleen models how to stretch out the word aloud. "What sound begins *sun*?" Lena offers the letter *s*. "What sound ends *sun*?" Jack offers the letter *n*. Both students came to the chart stand to write the letters. Kolleen left a blank line in between. "What's the middle sound? Think of the words *fun* and *run* and you'll know." Jordyn knows it is a *u* and comes up to write that word. Kolleen continues this process with words offered by the students: *flowers, butterfly, baseball,* and *ladybug*. Then, she asked the students to take some extra time to stretch out those hard words one syllable at a time and to think about all the sounds they need to write as letters.

That afternoon, Kolleen noticed a difference in the students' writing. She could read almost every piece without help from the authors. For a few students, she held a one-on-one conference to rethink the focus lesson. Here is the chart they created and posted in the room:

How We Spell the Words We Write

1. Say the word out loud two times.
2. Clap out the syllables.
3. Take each word part and stretch it out to listen for the sounds.
4. Blend the sounds together.
5. Look at the word you wrote.
6. Say the word out loud the way you wrote it.

Whole-Group Revision
Conference with
Third-Grade Writers
http://sten.pub/ac09

Kolleen called her writers together at the end of workshop. "You are doing a great job with your kid writing. The vowels are tricky, but you are showing me how much knowledge you have about the way sounds are spelled."

In spring, Brenda Krupp's third-grade class was working on a narrative unit of study and trying to write a story around a theme with a lesson learned. Brenda had asked her third graders to draw a smiley face in a place of their writing that they particularly liked. Sophia put her smiley face near her ending because she felt she had showed the emotions that let the reader know her characters were good friends. After hearing a few responses, she moved them to find a place where revision was needed—where the students felt they did not like the way their writing was going, where something wasn't working for them. Here, she referred to the anchor chart the students had created with her after they had planned and created their first draft. The students had contributed strategies from previous focus lessons, such as creating tension in their lead paragraph, changing lazy sentences into action sentences, changing fake talk into realistic dialogue, showing instead of telling, exact word choice, and endings. Turner noticed that by changing a lazy sentence into an action sentence, he had made his writing more concise. Audrey needed a way to make a door sound. Mya suggested that she should do some research—open a door and shut it. Other students gave an example. Brenda suggested that sometimes we just should just use the words: *The door opened.* She reminded them about creating a hook with tension. Sophia wanted to fix her lead with exact word choice. "Who can name me a lead she might want to try and maybe even a book she might use?" Ryan suggested starting with "It all started with . . . " And referred to the opening sentence in *Circus Mirandus*, a favorite read-aloud in this year's class. Brenda asked them to continue to think about the places they wanted to keep and the places they needed to revise. She referred to items on the anchor chart as a way to wrap things up. She specifically emphasized satisfying endings, recognizing that at this point in time, it was an area of need for many of them and asked them to help each other. The whole-group conference gave students a chance to share part of their stories they really liked and a part that they felt was not working for them. In addition, it gave Brenda a chance to review the qualities of writing on their anchor chart, the points they needed to pay attention to when they continued to work on their pieces. Finally, it instilled confidence, as well as a dose of stamina to continue the good work of revision. (See Figure 6.7.)

Figure 6.7
I Like This! I'm Struggling with This!

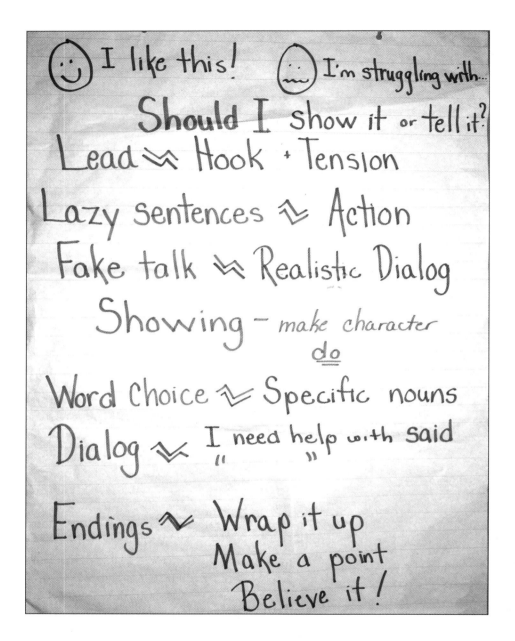

Whole-group conferences are a great way to use the entire community to wrestle with problems and to come up with viable solutions. Many heads are often better than one. One afternoon after lunch, Brenda gathered her writers on the carpet and posed this question: *What are the possibilities for our classroom to balance noise and quiet during workshop time?* Ideally, it would be great if students could all meet with their partners to confer at the same time. Although sometimes this can be accomplished on days when a conference clock is used to make "appointments" (see Chapter 9, "Quick and Easy"), it is not always possible to do this. Brenda was making time to assess a real classroom need. On most days, students in her classroom were in different stages of the writing process and had different needs. While some students were drafting, others were publishing or conferring. While some students needed quiet, others were eager to hold a peer conference, to share their published pieces, or to talk to another writer about topic selection or research issues. Brenda asked her students to turn and talk about solutions to this problem of noise versus quiet time in workshop. The students quickly grouped themselves in pairs, or threes and sometimes fours, and after five minutes of talk, Brenda asked for a whole-group share. To make their thinking visible and permanent, Brenda recorded their thoughts on an anchor chart and honored each contributor by placing his name after his comment. In this way, Brenda was also able to reflect on who was doing the talking and who was silent, how her students solved problems, what they knew to be true of writing workshop, and what they wanted to honor during this special time of day. Figure 6.8 lists their ideas:

Figure 6.8
Possibilities to Balance Noise and Quiet During Writing Workshop

---

1. Use the carpet if you want to talk about your stories. (Tammy and Audrey)
2. Be sure to use your whisper voices whenever you are on the carpet sharing. (Ryan and Jax)
3. Make a poster to display writing time when no one should be talking. (Turner)
   Questions and Comments: "How much time for that?" (Mya)
                          "Maybe five minutes?" (Timmy)
                          "I think more time is needed. Ten minutes." (Waylon)
4. If you are having a conference, use the library area. (Sophia)
   Comments: "I think only two people at a time. It's not a big area." (Sophia)
           "I think you can get two conference pairs in that space." (Dan)
           "We should test it out." (Bryce)
5. We can make some of the tables "quiet" tables for conferences. (Jax)
   Comment: "We could label them so we know where to go without asking Mrs. Krupp." (Claire)
6. There could be one table for publishing your work. (Ryan)
   Comment: "We could keep scissors, glue, colored pencils, paper, and markers there in a box." (Krissh)
7. Some tables have to be for planning and drafting. (Mia)
   Comment: "We could do our revision there before and after we have a conference." (Claire)
   Comment: "We could use the same table for editing or maybe use a desk or two in the hallway if only two people use that space." (JD)

The third graders made this plan work for the spring months until the close of school. Because they designed the physical environment, they were much more committed to making this balance happen. Brenda and Lynne noticed that, at first, the students sometimes walked closer to the anchor chart to review the physical plan. After a while they didn't need it anymore. The workshop was humming with the whisper of voices, the scratch-scratch of pencils traveling across yellow notepads, and the purr of notebook pages turned and read.

Our Final Thoughts

The power of reflection cannot be overemphasized. The student writers should be doing most of the talking in a conference. Here are a set of questions that may work for all conferences to engage students to reflect on their own processes:

- What strategies or craft moves did you try?
- What didn't work?
- What can you do differently the next time?
- Where do you feel you need more support (i.e., mini-lesson, conference, new mentor text, collaboration)?

With a colleague or grade-level team, take a few minutes to reflect on these questions:

1. Why do we hold writing conferences with our students? Brainstorm a list of reasons.
2. What types of conferences have you held in your writing classroom? What types will you try to use in the future?
3. When conferring with your students, what are the overall goals you hope to accomplish?
4. When you think about these goals, do they change based on the mode of writing you are teaching? Why or why not?
5. Think about the writing types (narrative, informational, opinion, poetry) or authors you study, and create an essential conference question or questions for each of these types or authors.
6. What different configurations (one on one, small group, whole group) do you use in your writing classroom? How do you decide which configuration to use?
7. How do conferences move our student writers toward greater independence?

Chapter 7

PEER CONFERENCES
A Chance to Grow, Share, and Receive Immediate Feedback

> " Remember that the writing workshop is a place where students learn how to live as writers and how to do what writers do. If we've got twenty-eight people in the room writing, that's twenty-eight ongoing demonstrations of how one might go about that, and students can learn from all of these demonstrations . . . they can learn from anyone. "

—Katie Wood Ray with Lester Laminack, *The Writing Workshop: Working Through the Hard Parts (And They're All Hard Parts)*

One factor of formative assessment in the writing workshop classroom is the application of student-to-student conferring. Sharing with a partner is nonthreatening for certain and with care and practice can provide the just-in-time feedback that gives a student writer the appropriate nudge forward needed. NCTE's Assessment Task Force, in their report "Formative Assessment That *Truly* Informs Instruction" states that good formative assessment "includes feedback that is non-evaluative, specific, timely, and related to the learning goals, and that provides opportunities for the student to revise and improve work products and deepen understandings" (2013, 3). In a writing workshop community, there is not just one teacher in the room. All writers think, write, react, and share. We believe that student writers can be helpful advisers to their fellow writers early in the year, but they do need modeling, as well as practice. Regie Routman (2005) advises that student writers need preparation to become effective peer conferrers. This preparation consists of observations of conferences led by their teacher, learning to ask thoughtful questions, practicing effective feedback during sharing time, and practice with teacher feedback.

Getting Started with Peer Conferences

Students must receive timely feedback as well as reflect on where they have been, where they presently are, and where they are headed with their writing goals. By training our students to be effective conference partners, we can make time for every student to share his piece and receive some feedback. Not only is this practice engaging and satisfying, it is a way to personalize learning and empower students by elevating them to a position of teacher or coach. Because class size is often too big to get to everyone in the course of a writing workshop period or even several periods, peer conferring offers a solution so some students do not become discouraged and give up. Writers need an audience, and peers provide one for them—safe, immediate, and, at times, motivational and inspirational. Overmeyer (2015, 83) suggests observing your students during peer conferences to find a pair who seem to be doing well and can serve as a model peer conference for the class. He asks the student pair to demonstrate (repeat their conference conversation or possibly have another one) and together, with the students, an anchor chart is created and labeled *A Successful Peer Conference*. Ackerman and McDonough (2016) also suggest creating an anchor chart, which they call an I-chart, to help students successfully navigate the peer conference. Students watched conferring videos of their classmates to discover what went well and what needed to be improved. After students viewed the videos, they came up with the following list (2016, 46):

1. I will look my partner in the eye.
2. I will sit next to my partner.
3. I will listen to my partner.
4. I will offer a compliment.
5. I will try to help.
6. I will stay on task.

A chart like this is useful to our youngest writers. Connections can be made with cooperative learning and social skills that are necessary to have a true interactive conversation. Here, you may want to take time to create a T-chart with two columns: *What a Peer Conference Looks Like* and *What a Peer Conference Sounds Like*. An M-chart would include *What a Peer Conference Feels Like*. These charts are created collaboratively as a whole-group process after students have participated in a few peer conferences. Talking about their experiences and charting their thinking help the student writers to own the process.

Read, Retell, Respond

We can learn a great deal to inform our writing instruction by listening in on our students when they confer with their peers. First, we prepare student writers to be helpful conferrers by offering them a process for success. A format for primary students in kindergarten and first grade is *read, retell, respond.* Students work in triads to share their writing and take on each role. As one person reads, another peer has the job of retelling what he hears the author say. This role helps students to develop active listening skills, keeping them focused on the task at hand. Retelling a story is often a skill practiced in reading workshop, so the connection here with writing workshop is a natural one. The third person in the triad responds by offering a specific praise. We ask our young writers to tell the student author what he has heard that stood out to him, gave him a picture in his mind, or connected with what the class had been studying in writing workshop. Here, students can notice a craft move, such as writing in the voice of an animal or an object, and praise peers for applying the work of mini-lessons documented in anchor charts. Then, the next cycle begins and everyone takes on a new role. By the third rotation, each writer has shared his story, retold someone else's story, and offered specific praise. During this time, a teacher can clipboard-cruise to listen in, to take notes about how the students are responding, and to listen for the tracks of her teaching within her young writers' stories.

Story Star Conference

Another great peer conference structure for primary students is the Story Star Peer Conference to sharpen focus and build content. Sue Mowery, a friend and colleague, spent twenty years traveling around the state of Pennsylvania to coach teachers on the structure and processes of reading and writing workshop. She used several oil cloths to create stars large enough for first graders to sit in. Then she gave sets of five students index cards she had laminated with one of the question markers on it: *Who, Where* and *When* (these questions were listed on the same index card), *What, How,* and *Why.* She chose a few students to be the Story Star authors, and, after a reading, she circulated around the group to whisper possible questions if students were stuck. The Story Star authors answered the questions and decided whether to add information to their writing piece. Through the first several tries, Sue recorded questions for these authors on chart paper or the board to help them remember and possibly consider using for revision purposes. The Story Star format can also be used for students to orally rehearse a story before they write. This conference format is a solid way to observe students and assess their ability to ask appropriate questions to move a piece forward. The key is to make the connection to their own writing and to realize they should be asking themselves questions as a way to revise their writing before coming to a peer or a teacher conference.

Notice, Ponder, Polish

Often, we like to use the *notice, ponder, polish* format. *Notice* what the writer has done well and explain why you think so. *Ponder*: ask a question (see anchor chart: *Kinds of Questions to Ask Writers* in Chapter 4). *Polish*: suggest a change the writer might make to explore the possibilities of the piece. We share our own writing as well as writing from student volunteers to help us to implement the format for our student writers, practicing one item at a time.

First, we notice what the writer did well: "I noticed that your piece starts in the middle of the game with the crowd cheering. That really got me involved in the action right away." Or "I noticed you used onomatopoeia several times in your piece. Sometimes writers go overboard with sounds, but your piece seemed just right. I noticed that each time you used onomatopoeia it was purposeful. For example, the cheering of the crowd, and the sound of the bat, both brought me right beside you in the stands." "I like what you wrote " is a comment that will not help the writer, because the writer doesn't know what exactly the reader found interesting or helpful or "good," but stating specifically *what* in the piece sticks with the reader will help. The responder, whether teacher or peer, does not comment on the writer's ability but on the product and the effort the writer used to achieve the effect.

In her groundbreaking work *Mindset: The New Psychology of Success*, Carol S. Dweck (2006, 72) says that praising students for doing what they need to do to succeed produces a growth mind-set, whereas praising students for their abilities has a largely negative effect. When the writer hears what the reader/listener enjoyed about the piece, it is likely that she will replicate the strategy in future pieces. Thus, writers become mentors for other writers and also for themselves. Dweck tells us that the outcome can be praised as long as you make sure you also talk about the process that led to that outcome. She suggests these areas of praise:

- Effort
- Struggle
- Applying strategies
- Taking risks
- Seeking input
- Improvement
- Persistence
- Progress toward long-term and short-term goals
- Evidence of learning

The *ponder* part of the strategy is often the most difficult for student writers to implement. We spend time modeling the kinds of questions to ask writers. We pose questions that ask for more information (*Can you tell me more about the setting? What else can you tell me about the people who were there with you? What happened when you went back to the dugout?*). We ask questions to clear up what we don't understand (*I'm confused by this part where you say you were alone because earlier you talked about friends who were with you. When did they leave? Or, I'm not sure I understand why it is important for us to know that you do not like to eat lima beans.*). We ask questions when we need more specificity (*Where did this take place? Who was with you? How did you feel about what happened? Is this a place you know really well—can you add to the description to help us see it better?*). We ask for examples (*Can you compare the ice cream sundae to something else to help us recognize how big it was?*). We ask questions about the ending (*Did you consider any other endings? What effect did you want your ending to have?*). Notice that some of these questions can lead to polish and, therefore, serve as a "two-fer." For example, if you ask the writer, "Is it important to know that you don't like lima beans?" and the writer realizes it has nothing to do with his piece, then he eliminates it to make the writing tighter and clearer.

We end with suggestions (polish) for the writer: *I notice that many of your sentences begin the same way: "I was; I saw; then I saw; I did." What do you think you can do so that your sentences have some variety? Do you remember when we combined sentences from* Saturdays and Teacakes? *Could you try that out here? Or I see that you use a lot of adverbs to describe your verbs, like "walked quickly, and talked fast." How could you change the verb to say "walked quickly"?* Writers then decide whether to use the suggestion. We stress that the writing is theirs; they are the decision makers. When we listen in on our peer conferrers, we discover not only what they know (or don't know) about conferring but also what they believe constitutes effective writing. (See Appendix 6, "Notice, Ponder, Polish Conferences.")

 SPOTLIGHT ON FORMATIVE ASSESSMENT

Conferring with Second Graders

Students in my second-grade class are working on revising their pieces and are focusing on their word choices. Sharing mentor texts that have vivid verbs and adjectives helps my students revise their own work. However, there are times they are stuck and can't seem to find a word that shows the shade of meaning they want for their piece.

Hannah was working on a circular structure piece and came to conference with me about word choices. I noticed she used the words get and see several times. We read her piece together and highlighted these words. Hannah laughed, and said, "Oh my, I didn't notice that I used them so much until I highlighted them." I challenged her to go back and reread her piece and to grab the thesaurus to help find other words that convey the meaning she is searching for.

Examples of her revisions:

Before: When the train starts going he will see a meadow.
After: When the train starts chugging along he will spot a meadow.

Before: He will see cows.
After: He will notice cows.

Before: He'll go and ask the conductor to stop the train.
After: He'll pull the emergency brake and bound toward the meadow.

Lily was working on her circular story as well. We read her piece together, and we noticed she used "she will" several times in her piece. She highlighted all the examples in her draft. We discussed sentence fluency in her piece. I asked if she could start her sentences differently instead of using "she will."
She went back to her desk, and here are her changes.

Before: She will ask you to get it.
After: She asks you to buy it.

Before: When you give it to her she will see a big sign that says ball dancing today at the town square.
After: When you give her the dress she notices a big sign . . .

Before: She will dance for five or six hours and she will be so thirsty.
After: After dancing for five or six hours, her thirst is real!

Before: She will order a chocolate milkshake with chocolate chips.
After: She orders a chocolate milkshake with chocolate chips and a dash of whipped cream.

In April, we were working on Earth Day poems, and we were focusing on our senses. I have done so much with visualization in reading and writing, and I wanted to see how this transferred to their writing. I find asking questions is very beneficial when conferencing with students. Justin's Earth Day poem was lacking details and it was difficult to visualize his intentions. Together, we read the poem and I wrote on a sticky note some questions for him to consider when he went back to his desk.

Before: I feel cool air on a summer day.
Questions: What are you doing on a summer day? What are you playing?
After: I feel cool air on a summer day playing in the park.

Before: I hear birds chirping and wind blowing.
Questions: What kind of birds and can you compare the wind blowing to something you are familiar with?
After: I hear robins chirping and wind blowing like an ocean breeze.

My goal is to help my students learn how to be good question makers, and to be able to ask questions of their peers and of themselves when they confer. I model as often as possible. The students are noticing how the questioning has led them to revise for detail and stronger word choice. Their writing becomes more specific with each revision attempt. They can see themselves growing as writers!

Beth Stump is a second-grade teacher at Kutztown Elementary School in Kutztown Area School District in Kutztown, Pennsylvania.

Third Graders Engage in Peer Conferences

Brenda Krupp and Kevin Black create opportunities for students to confer with one another on a daily basis. They understand that their students grow as writers, in self-esteem and in skill, from making smart choices about their pieces and by reflecting on what worked and what still needs tweaking. Practicing the close reading of a text by listening and sometimes viewing the writing of peers in the writing community helps students monitor and adjust their own writing.

Brenda's third graders were experts at peer conferences. They developed their own set of strategies as they held a conference. Consider this conference between Dan and Bryce. Bryce is writing a story called "The Basketball Challenge." He asks Dan to listen as he reads his beginning of the action. He's already had a conference with Dan about his lead paragraph and made some changes to tighten it up (see Figure 7.1a and 7.1b). Bryce reads his piece to Dan and asks him to talk about what he likes. Dan liked the action, especially the image of the tsunami, and suggests shortening a bit to get to the main action of the story sooner. He is concerned that Bryce's readers may get lost and miss the point that is coming. Bryce agrees and asks Dan to read part of the story with him. When the boys finish reading the piece aloud, they talk about the tsunami image, which will definitely be in Bryce's final piece. Bryce tries it out and then uses an arrow to move the sentence to a new position. He shows Dan and suggests the addition of an ellipsis before the sound words and adds a sticky note to mark its location in the text. When Bryce writes his final draft, he will make a decision whether to use Dan's suggestions. (See Appendix 7, "Ways to Respond.")

Third Graders Dan and Bryce
Hold a Peer Conference
http://sten.pub/ac10

Figure 7.1a
A Section of Bryce's Draft for
"The Basketball Challenge"

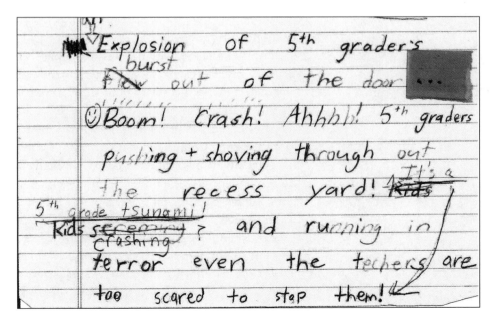

Figure 7.1b
Bryce's Final Draft for "The Basketball Challenge"

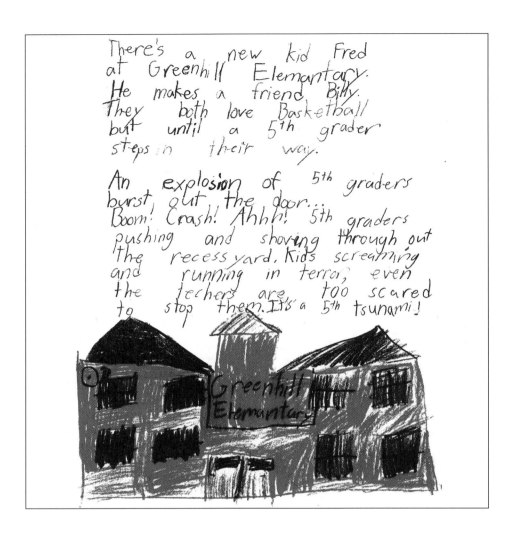

There's a new kid Fred at Greenhill Elemantary. He makes a friend Billy. They both love Basketball but until a 5th grader steps in their way.

An explosion of 5th graders burst out the door... Boom! Crash! Ahhh! 5th graders pushing and shoving through out the recess yard. Kids screaming and running in terror, even the techers are too scared to stop them. It's a 5th tsunami!

Greenhill Elemantary

Third graders in Kevin's classroom had been working hard preparing for the state writing test, so he decided that they should have some fun writing an imaginative narrative. They brainstormed possible topics, reviewed features of narrative, and set to work. After most students had drafted, Kevin suggested that they confer about their drafts with a classroom peer. He reminded them of the procedure, using the classroom anchor charts as reference.

Typically, the conference begins with the writer reading her draft. Then, the responder notices, ponders, and suggests polish. Listening in on Skylar and Zen conferring on Skylar's sports piece, Kevin made notes. Zen noticed about Skylar's piece: "You kept it short, but not too short. You used details." As his teacher, Kevin recognized that Zen made a specific observation, but he did not mention what counted as a detail nor how the addition of the detail made the piece more interesting. *Was he able to picture the field? Were these "showing" details?* Kevin made a note to address this omission in a future focus lesson. Student writers and peer responders need to recognize the importance of details (content) in all genres of writing. Is Zen's response typical of his class-

Zen and Skylar Hold a Peer
Conference, Grade Three
http://sten.pub/ac11

Sarah and Michaela Confer,
Grade Three
http://sten.pub/ac12

Maggie and Addie in a
Peer Conference
http://sten.pub/ac13

mates? A focus lesson during writing workshop is one way to find out. Next, Zen questioned Skylar about the absence of characters. "Could you put in more characters?" Skylar answered that question with his reason for not including more people. "I didn't want my piece to get confusing." Skylar worried that too many characters would make the piece unwieldy. Skylar recognizes that a narrative needs to have a focus and that focus can be lost when a piece gets too big. Finally, Zen made a suggestion regarding polish, which he asks in the form of a question: "What did the coach say? Readers might want to know that especially if they don't know the game." Zen is thinking of readers other than himself and asks Skylar to think of them, too. Teaching points from this conference include a focus lesson on what counts as a detail, as well as focus. Listening in on the peer conference informed instruction for another day.

Michaela and Sarah confer on their pieces, too. Michaela asks Sarah why she used variation in print. Sarah explains her reasoning. This exchange is important because it shows that Sarah recognizes that variations in print is a technique that works to highlight an effect. Is this technique one others in the class employ? Sarah could be an expert resource for this particular strategy. As a responder to Michaela, Sarah is quite specific: "Can you tell me more about the setting? I noticed that many of your sentences have about the same number of words." Sarah doesn't tell Michaela what to do, but points out what she needs as the reader/listener.

Listening in on this conference, Kevin notes the successes and the misses. For example, Michaela's comment to Sarah, "That was really good!" is not particularly helpful. What, specifically, did Sarah think was "good"? Sarah, on the other hand, points out Michaela's lack of sentence variety, that many of her sentences begin in the same way and have a similar number of words. Kevin makes a note to remind student conferrers to be specific.

In another peer conference, Kevin notes that Maggie is quite self-assured and forceful in her comments. Maggie compliments Addie on her organization, but she doesn't say why the organization is effective. It's chronological order. Why is that a good way to organize this piece? She also suggests adding characters, but why are more characters needed? Addie does not respond to either comment. As Kevin listens in on the conference, he notes that Maggie is a strong responder and that when Addie offers suggestions, Maggie is willing to implement them. These are important facts for their teacher to recognize, especially when pairing student writers for conferences or when using conferring as a demonstration and sharing session. Yet, a need exists for reteaching and modeling specific feedback (particularly with regard to Maggie's organizational comment).

Kevin listens in on the conferences, taking notes (*Details: What are they specifically in this piece? How did they help? Audience—consider the audience. What might they know and not know?*). As Kevin continues to listen in, he compiles notes to refer to in planning future lessons. He also notes which students may be classroom resource experts (*Sarah—variation in print, for example*). As students confer with their fellow writers, they become resources and experts. They gain confidence in themselves as writers, too. Classroom teachers cannot listen in on every conference, of course. In upper grades, conference sheets can be used for accountability and for teachers to see what kinds of responses are being offered. (See notice, ponder, polish response forms in Appendixes 8 and 9.) As writing teachers, we continually monitor and adjust our mini- and focus lessons to accommodate our student writers' needs.

Creating Partnerships Between Classrooms: Fifth Graders Confer with Second Graders

Megan, Grade Two, and Devyn, Grade Five, Partner for a Peer Conference http://sten.pub/ac14

In Dawn Costello's second-grade classroom, students have a unique opportunity to engage in peer conferences with Dan Monaghan's fifth graders. On this particular visit, Lynne observed three fifth graders walking into Dawn's classroom without Dan. The two classes had come together for peer conferring once or twice a month since the fall. Dawn's class was learning to insert "from here to there" as a craft move for the narratives they were writing about "The Worst Day Ever!" or "The Best Day Ever!" after listening to *Alexander and the Terrible, Horrible, No Good, Very Bad Day.* The students had spent some time brainstorming, and most were eager to write *worst day* stories. Dawn thought that Judith Viorst had inspired them with her humor. She also encouraged students to think about their scariest, happiest, or most embarrassing day so they had more freedom of topic. They had the option of writing a story of their choice, but Viorst's story delighted them and many chose to use the "very bad day" idea. That week, Dawn had also returned to revisit *Down The Road* by Alice Schertle to show how a writer uses transition words and punctuation to move from one place to the next. Megan read her entire piece to her fifth-grade partner, Devyn, and then asked Devyn to listen for her "here to there" and a satisfying ending. To make the peer conference easier for both the second and fifth graders, Dawn and Dan trained the writers to first read the whole piece while the responder just listened to get a feel for the content. Next, the reader shared the narrative in stages, stopping after the beginning, the middle, and the end to receive feedback and to jot down a few words or phrases.

As you can see, the girls worked well together, both listening to each other. Devyn recorded on a sticky note to give to Megan when the conference was over. Devyn praised Megan's setting detail (*the big, white fan*) that helped her form a picture in her mind, her word choice of *cashier*, and her satisfying ending, a hope, wish, or dream for the future. Megan chose to do some revision to clarify the scene. She added a question to extend her thought shot. *Did Mom leave the store?* The peer conference gave Megan a chance to share her work and to receive immediate feedback, and it gave Devyn a chance to lead a writerly life and mentor her partner with her noticings and a question that led to a polish. The fifth grader's easygoing manner and self-confidence was also noted. To have this kind of flow in conference, it was evident that the fifth grader was writing every day and immersed in writing workshop practices. Also, Devyn was a reader. She noted that it was a good thing that Megan's character was not flat but had changed from beginning to end, as the scary feelings of being lost transformed into tears of joy as Megan was reunited with her mom. Megan's story may suggest future opportunities to further explore, using mentor texts, the roller coaster of emotions a main character can experience. (See Figure 7.2.)

Figure 7.2
Megan's "The Worst Day Ever!" Story

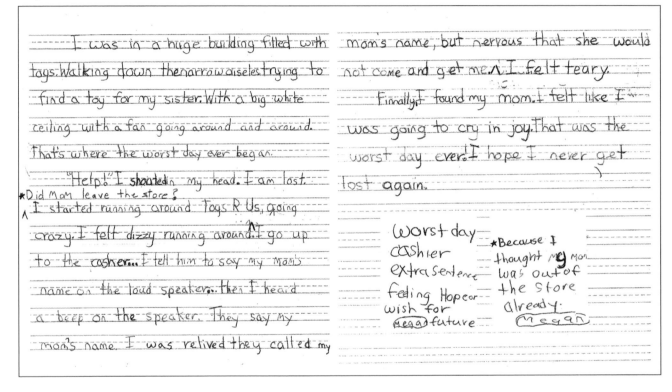

Casey conferred with second grader Abigail about her *worst day ever* story and followed the same routine.

Abigail read her entire story to Casey and then proceeded to break it up into a sectional read of beginning, middle, and end. Abigail asked Casey to listen for details she could add. Both teachers practice this routine: to ask your partner to listen for one or two specific things if possible and make suggestions. Casey noticed the detailed description of setting to open the narrative. After Abigail shared the middle, Casey surprised Lynne by asking Abigail if she was alone in the lost and found. Her advice to use show, not tell by talking about butterflies in your stomach rather than just saying she was sad was sound advice. As Casey states, "It tells you're nervous without actually telling people you're nervous." As you can see on Abigail's sticky note, she is considering

revising to add a detail about the lost and found and the show, not tell. Casey ends on a positive note, noticing that Abigail's ending links with her beginning where she talked about Disney characters. She states matter-of-factly that when Abigail names Disney World in her closing paragraph, it helps the reader figure out where this story took place if there was any doubt. (See Figure 7.3.)

Figure 7.3
Abigail's "The Worst Day Ever!" Story

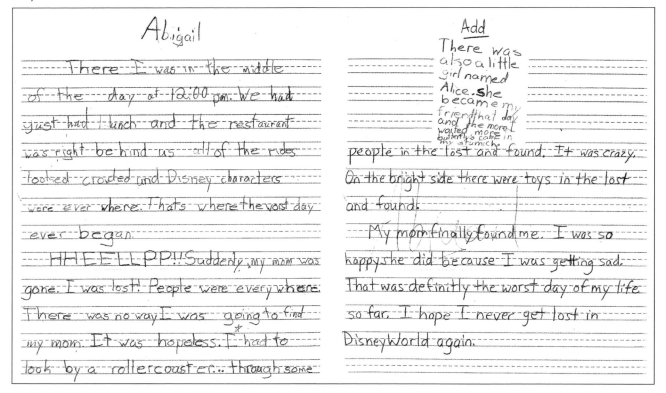

It is not the job of peer conferrers to fix everything. Peer conferences give young writers another audience, another ear to listen carefully and notice a few places where the writer shines, perhaps to ask a question to clarify or satisfy the reader/listener's curiosity, and then give a suggestion or two for revision possibilities. In peer conferences, the writer has the final say and must decide whether to use the suggestions from his peers. He may, indeed, choose not to use any. It is very freeing and empowering to the writer to have that control. Often, in a student-teacher conference, the expectation, even if unspoken, is to try out a suggestion offered by the teacher.

Mark Overmeyer (2015) will ask students to model a peer conference for the entire class so the class can talk about the advice that is offered. Overmeyer suggests that, at first, peers may be better at asking questions than giving advice. When the whole class gets together to reflect on the work they've accomplished in writing workshop, they can share questions and tips that helped them revise their pieces.

Another by-product of peer conferences is the nurturing of writing identities. When we ask students to share their work with others; to help each other move forward with noticings, questions, and suggestions; and then to revise their work, we are growing their writing identities, focusing on their growth as a writer, not on the individual piece of writing they happen to be working on at that moment.

Listening for the Language of Writers: Student-to-Student Conferences

Children, in their own ways, teach us about the language of our classrooms. The teacher has to make something of what children say and do. Making sense of the oral language we use and its impact on creating student success was the motivation for the conversations about peer conferences. The work conducted in the discussions evolved from a need to discover how language affects student learning. Lynne began on a journey of talk.

The concept of multilayering mentoring was the aha moment that came to light to frame the questions for guided instructional conversations between a literacy coach and teacher. This subsequently led to action plans with goals and steps to define the process. Well-formulated goals lead to action; they offer more than hopes and wishes.

For Lynne, the essential question was: How do coaching conversations about information gathered during student writing conferences impact teacher instructional decisions? Dawn and Kelly, two second-grade teachers, asked this question: How can I get my students to hold effective peer conferences? All agreed one of the most difficult skills to develop is the specific language writers need to support other writers during peer conferences. Setting the stage called for some preparatory work. The recursive conversations presented several challenges.

Our Final Thoughts

In a writing workshop community, there is not just one teacher in the room. All writers think, write, react, and share. Student writers can be helpful advisers to their fellow writers early in the year, but they do need modeling, as well as practice. Students must receive quick feedback. They must reflect on where they have been, where they presently are, and where they are headed in their writing goals. How do we help our student writers become helpful conferrers? First, we offer them a process for success by modeling what a successful conference looks and sounds like. For young writers, we begin with read, retell, respond. The notice (praise), ponder, polish format is useful for second through middle school grades.

What can we notice?

- We notice a sharp focus—the writer did not stray from his intended path.
- We notice elaboration, the details—the writer offers examples, descriptions, explanations.
- We notice organizational scaffolds—use of transition words, strong leads, effective endings.
- We notice word choice—exact nouns, strong verbs, use of imagery.
- We notice sentence fluency—varying lengths and patterns.
- We praise effective punctuation.

What can we ponder (question)?

- Ask for more information to remove ambiguity or generalizations.
- Ask the direction of the piece—where is the reader headed?—if the focus isn't sharp.
- Ask the writer to tell you what the most important part of the piece is (helps to clear up focus issues).
- Ask for examples or explanations to make the details clearer.
- Ask for a definition of an unfamiliar term.
- Ask for emotions when there is no evidence by telling or showing.
- Ask how the writer is planning to end the piece if it doesn't already have one.

What can we polish?

- Concentrate on word choice (strong nouns and verbs).
- Sentence fluency—a variety of long and short sentences that begin different ways, suggesting sentence combining when appropriate.
- What can we add or change to give this piece voice or to make this piece sound like the writer?
- Add description to appeal to the senses—a piece is usually better when two senses are used rather than only one (such as sight).
- Use of transitional devices and organizational scaffolds (*When I was young in the mountains . . .*).
- Use of more sophisticated punctuation (colon, semicolon, parentheses, ellipses, quotation marks).
- Literary devices—similes, metaphors, personification, hyperbole, alliteration.

In whole-group share, decide what will be shared in whole group ahead of time: an unexpected praise that someone gave you, something you did not know you did, a polish that you will use, a suggestion you gave to a peer, a revision or edit you made because of a peer suggestion. As you observe your student during peer conferences and listen to the writerly talk during the final reflection, you might want to consider these questions to help you assess your students' needs and growth.

- Which students are able to use their knowledge of writing traits to talk about the qualities of writing?
- Which students can be grouped together for instructional purposes?
- Which students are willing to take risks and which are not?
- What are students capable of doing independently?
- Which students are resistant to letting other people's thinking influence their writing decisions?

Peer conferences are one of the most effective ways to grow writers. Mostly, we find that students find it easy to talk writer to writer in a peer conference. They are not threatened by their peers' suggestions and may use all or part of them. Peer conferences give our writers an audience on a daily basis—a chance to be recognized as a writer, to receive a few pats on the back, and support to move forward. Peer conferences are a positive, effective way for the entire writing community to move forward.

Chapter 8

SELF-ASSESSMENT
Opportunities for Reflection

" Serious writing requires long thinking . . . It takes reflection, the courage to dive below the surface, the willingness to live with a topic for a long period of time, turn it over and over in your mind, and decide for yourself what questions to ask about it. "

—Vicki Spandel, *The 9 Rights of Every Writer: A Guide for Teachers*

In classrooms across the United States, students have grown accustomed to listening to what is perceived as a strength in their work (whether it is work in writing workshop or other subject areas) and what is an area targeted for improvement. If we want our students to be a part of the assessment process and learn how to reflect on their writing, then we must look for a different classroom routine. In these classrooms, students practice reflection to improve their awareness and analysis of their own thinking processes (metacognition). A natural consequence is that they engage in a struggle with the quality of their writing pieces, viewing the writing process as recursive instead of linear, and embedding revision and editing across the process and as early as the prewriting (planning) stage.

If we focus on our students as essential evaluators in their process, then we are promising them one of the best opportunities that a classroom can afford—the opportunity to be part of their entire literacy journey. We must ask ourselves: What are the most effective practices we can use to help students make successful decisions about their writing? By examining how we delegate student responsibility for self-assessment and ongoing reflection, we can determine what is working for our students and for us, what new strategies we may choose to adapt, and what value our students place on reflection as a part of the learning process.

If our priority goal is to teach our students *how* to learn instead of *what* to learn, then we must recognize that students cannot carve out their own pathways (directions) if they are not regularly engaging in self-reflection. When students engage in a close reading of their work for purposes of self-assessment and reflection, they are making choices about what to keep and what to change. They are in control. After the mini-lesson, Lynne always posts one or two reflection questions on the whiteboard or chart paper. She reads them to the students just before they begin their independent writing time. The students know that the last two to five minutes of workshop will be about reflection. Lynne calls them to the rug by the chart stand to share strategies that worked, problem-solving attempts that failed, new questions, and new discoveries. Sometimes, the students will just read a small part of the piece they are working on, for example, their satisfying ending for their narrative to link with the mini-lessons for this week. Scheduling time to reflect at the end of each writing workshop will help students to understand its value. Starr Sackstein asserts, "Ultimately, we want students to become thoughtful lifelong learners who don't need to be reminded to reflect on the events of their lives" (2015b, 34). Another way we can create opportunities for reflection is to teach students how to engage in self-conferences.

Self-Conferences

We want our student writers to have many opportunities to write, to confer, and to think about their writing. We want our student writers to make decisions about their pieces and to be reflective about those decisions. No one knows a piece of writing as well as the writer of that piece. As teachers, we can never know what our students know how to do unless we ask them to tell us what they believe they have done well, what they have worked hard at trying, and what they think they need to do to improve their writing. Student writers, even in the primary grades, need to engage in self-evaluation, for this is how writers become independent practitioners. As they reflect on their writing, student writers begin to recognize their strengths and own up to their weaknesses, resulting in goal setting that comes from self-knowledge. That self-knowledge is the result of understanding the specifics of the skill of writing. In *Hacking Assessment* (2015a), Sackstein makes clear that reflection helps students become better learners. We, of course, agree.

Self-evaluation does not happen magically. Students need to learn to reflect through practice. We encourage students to be reflective by making reflection part of the writing workshop: *What did you write today that you are proud of? What did you work hard at today? What did you learn about writing opinion today?* Students may pair with a partner to share their answers to these questions, write responses in their writer's notebook, or share their thoughts with the whole class. If we believe self-assessment and reflection are valuable, we make time for them in our daily practice.

Checklists for Self-Assessment

A quick way to provide a scaffold for students to self-confer is a simple checklist. (See Chapter 3, "Checklists and Rubrics," for additional examples.) As they compare their written pieces to the items on the checklist, students begin the process of evaluating their product. However, a checklist does not necessarily encourage writers to reflect about what they have accomplished or what they have yet to achieve. A natural opportunity for such reflection and conferring can come at the end of a unit of study. For example, in Kevin Black's third-grade classroom in the spring, Kevin asked the class to go back to their writer's notebooks and to their drafts and revisions to complete some open-ended responses:

> Something I wrote that I like . . .
>
> I like this because . . .
>
> Something I tried hard at . . .
>
> I will try to improve my work by . . .

Responses to these sentence starters revealed self-awareness in the student writers. Sarah, for example, is quite specific about what she likes about her writing:

> **Something I wrote that I like** *Suddenly the park goes silent. No one can even hear a mouse chirping, and they're off!*
>
> **I like this because** I feel that it was very descriptive, and I really liked that.
>
> **Something I tried hard at**—I really tried hard to entertain the reader and not to bore the reader or myself.
>
> **I will try to improve my work by** trying new words. For example, I think that I wrote to [sic] much of the word *suddenly*.

Sarah notes that description is her strong suit. She wants to entertain the reader, and she doesn't want to bore herself as the writer either. She also notices that she overuses the word *suddenly*. Word choice is an important component of good writing, and Sarah realizes that. Her reflection indicates that she knows that vivid description and exact words help bring a piece of writing to life. During this unit of study, she worked hard to incorporate these elements into her writing.

Julie says that she liked her piece on what school was like for colonial children. She notes that, when she shared her writing, the class responded that it "made them feel like they lived back then." That response made her realize that she had written a piece that connected with the reader. She says, though, that one thing she will do to improve her work is to give more examples, enriching her pieces by providing more details.

Gillian writes that she likes the phrase "so twisty" to describe a roller coaster, because she thinks it is "very funny." She recognizes the importance of word choice and says, "My word choice needs to be improve[d]."

Jim's favorite piece of writing is an opinion piece, "Should pets be allowed in school?" He liked writing it, "because it involves pets," and he "thought hard about what I was going to write." He says he needs to work on "going back to double check that I have all my facts."

The third graders continued to reflect on their progress as writers. They said such things as, "I know what to write about now: I have topics from my authority list and from my drawings" (Zen). "I like it more—it's fun for us because we have examples and models and mentor texts" (Skylar). "Writing got easier for me because we learned how to use strategies. I used to say 'Do I have to?' Now I say, 'Can't we write more?'" (Molly). "I feel like I'm a better writer. I use my imagination more" (Colson). When Diane and Kevin asked the students to take a "walk" through their writer's notebooks and reflect on what they noticed, students mentioned the following: "I'm better at noticing spelling." "I use more sentence variety." "I have longer pieces." "I have filled up more than one writer's notebook." "My work is neater." "My writing has better word choice and variety." "I don't over think—I have fun with my writing." "I like opinion now—I can do it." "I like to write information pieces—I remember a lot."

These glimpses into student self-evaluation are instructive for teachers. When we see what students value in their own writing, we are better conferrers, better coaches, better writing teachers. Looking at what student writers say about their own writing, indeed, giving them the opportunity and authority to make decisions about what works for them, is an important factor of formative assessment. How will we teachers make decisions about what our student writers need from us if we don't allow them to tell us what works for them? Self-evaluation is how our students communicate both their process and their product.

Self-Awareness Opportunities

To grow a reflective community, we need to provide many kinds of opportunities for reflection. Sharing our reflection with others may be as simple as posing a question and giving students time to think, ink, pair, share. In Kelly Gallagher's second-grade classroom, Kelly asked her students this question: *When are* you *a writer?* The students' responses were posted on an anchor chart. The variety of responses was telling and helped Kelly imagine situations in which the different kinds of writing might be used in writing workshop and across the day. Kelly talked with Lynne about the genres that are not commonly represented in mini-lesson instruction during writing workshop, such as writing jokes and riddles or lyrics for songs. "That doesn't mean we can't build in some help during an individual or small-group conference," Kelly mused. "If one of my students wants to create a holiday recipe book or write instructions for an imagined board or video game, that student should be encouraged to do exactly that. I hope that I can nurture my students' love for writing by promoting the creation of writing pieces that do not always fall neatly into narrative, opinion, and informational writing." Lynne agreed. Figure 8.1 shows one of three pages of the anchor chart Kelly created from her second graders' responses.

Lynne valued this conversation with Kelly. After working as a writing coach in elementary grades for many years, Lynne knew that sometimes our efforts to meet curricular demands do not always steer us in the direction of providing choice in writing workshop. Looking at a student's writer's notebook often reveals writing topics and genres we never get around to talking about— science fiction stories, comic strips, letters to family members, even the start of a graphic novel or picture book! The act of writing should be joyful. Writing

Figure 8.1
When Are You a Writer?

is, in many ways, a celebration. Even though there is hard work involved and many challenges, students will be more engaged if they feel they have some control. Choosing their topic, genre, work options (composing alone or in collaboration with others), and publication design can give students a sense of empowerment. In their experiences, inside and outside of school, there are not often opportunities to take charge. That's the beauty of writing workshop. It puts the students in the driver seat! Using a question like the one Kelly posed to gain insights into what students may be writing outside of your classroom may help you assess your writing curriculum and instruction, perhaps allowing you to build in time to honor their interests in our writing workshop. You could simply hold a writerly conversation or ask them to write you a letter about what kinds of writing they do in their free time or what kinds of writing would they like to try with support from you. Providing students with all kinds of notepaper to choose from is a good way to stimulate interest in writing to you about what interests them. Allowing them to customize their notepaper on the computer, or add drawings with colored pencil, or perhaps by gluing scraps of construction paper or fabric on their notepaper may be enough to get everyone writing a note to you about something they enjoy or would like to try. Is it worth the effort? Yes! This information will help you plan and revise your instruction to meet the needs of all your students, particularly those students who are not eager to write or who appear to be disinterested or struggling.

Older students can raise their self-awareness about feelings for writing and what they've learned from their writing pieces, craft moves, useful strategies, and mentor texts through websites, such as Weebly, Edublog, or WordPress, as well as Twitter and Instagram. Sometimes, our students spend more time composing reflections when they know a larger community will read their thoughts. We can also model the ways we offer reflection, not only in the classroom but also in our own blog posts, tweets, and publications. Lynne and Diane regularly post on their blogs. Lynne also posts a "Teacher to Teacher" piece six times a year for pawlpblog.org, the blog of the Pennsylvania Writing and Literature Project. When we write and reflect on our process and product, we can honestly and expertly model reflection for our students. How will you answer the question, *When are you a writer?*

SPOTLIGHT ON FORMATIVE ASSESSMENT

Author's Note: Best Practice Formative Assessment

Assessing writing—formative versus summative assessments—which is more meaningful? Which is more useful to teachers and learners? Which writing should be graded? When should it be graded? What is important about assessment?

Here's what I believe matters most in assessment: the writer's personal reflection about her writing. I teach my young writers to write author's notes at the end of their writing pieces. I want reflection to become an ongoing habit, not only after writers complete their pieces but also during their creation. If writers are composing, constructing, and crafting lengthy poems over the course of a few days, for example, I want them to begin composing an author's note during the process. When they publish, they can modify their thinking and reflection in the final author's note. This author's note becomes a kind of personal assessment. When a writer discusses the reason for her use of out-of-place adjectives for an intended effect, her thinking is self-assessment at its highest level. It gives us, the teachers of writers, the best possible insight into the thinking of that writer.

Reflection also gives us a way to assess our writers on a level that elevates what we can do with a simple (and often limited) rubric. The best writers make purposeful decisions about their composing, constructing, and crafting. If we, for example, are trying to assess "style" as a writing trait, we need to be aware of the element of subjectivity involved in assessing style. For example, the assessor may not accept the use of fragments no matter how purposeful. However, reading the writer's commentary in which their decision to construct a sentence fragment as an artful way to express a thought for an intended effect allows assessment at a more thoughtful level. This kind of assessment is both formative and summative. It's best practice!

Following are two examples of written pieces with author's notes from sixth-grade writers. What do the author's notes tell us about what the students know and are able to do?

Madi's Notebook Entry

Off the beach there was a shimmering ocean in the sunlight.
Off the beach there was an ocean, shimmering in the sunlight.

Author's note: *In class Mr. Murphy taught us about "out-of-place-adjectives" and how you can make an adjective pop out of the sentence to make it more powerful! The sentences are basically like play dough because you have to play with the sentences just like you play with play dough to make an "out-of-place-adjective."*

I made this sentence to create an image in your mind about an ocean shimmering, and make the "shimmering" next to the ocean an "out-of-place-adjective." Whenever I think of an ocean I think of how it shimmers in the sunlight. I really enjoyed learning about this in language arts because you get to craft your own sentences and make it your own.

Megan's Poem

so much depends
upon
a velvety stuffed
lamb
touched by defeat
filled with hope
now lingering beside the other
memories of my past

Author's note: *My stuffed lamb was given to me by my grandmother when I was a baby in the hospital. She gave it to me because her first toy was a stuffed lamb. I was born about four months early and my parents were told that I wouldn't live, and that if I managed to live I would have some type of mental disorder and/or other medical conditions. Today I live with no medical issues. I believe that my stuffed lamb helped me make it through the tough times in the hospital, and in the end defy the expectations that the doctors placed in my parents' heads. This poem was inspired by William Carlos Williams's poem "The Red Wheelbarrow." I separated each phrase to make them more dramatic. I believe that this "short but sweet" poem allows the reader to stay interested throughout the entire poem, it also allows the poem to sound crisp and powerful instead of making it sound like it is running on and going off topic.*

These notes reveal the thinking of their authors and show me, their teacher, what they value, what they know how to do, and what they are thinking. These insights are important not only to the writers who write them but to me, their teacher, as well.

Frank Murphy has taught for more than twenty-four years, currently in the Council Rock School District in Bucks County, Pennsylvania. He is the author of several popular Step into Reading History Readers, including the Oppenheimer Toy Portfolio 2006 Best Book Award Winner *Ben Franklin and the Magic Squares*. His latest book is *Take a Hike, Teddy Roosevelt!*

Surveys for Ongoing Reflection and Goal Setting

Figure 8.2 (left)
Jim, Grade Three End-of-the-Year Survey

Figure 8.3 (right)
Sarah, Grade Three End-of-the-Year-Survey

Kevin Black asked the third graders to reflect on how their attitudes toward writing had evolved over the course of the year by revisiting the attitude survey *My Feelings About Writing*. Jim's attitude toward writing has changed considerably since October (Figure 8.2), while Sarah, who already had positive feelings about writing, created new categories (Figure 8.3)!

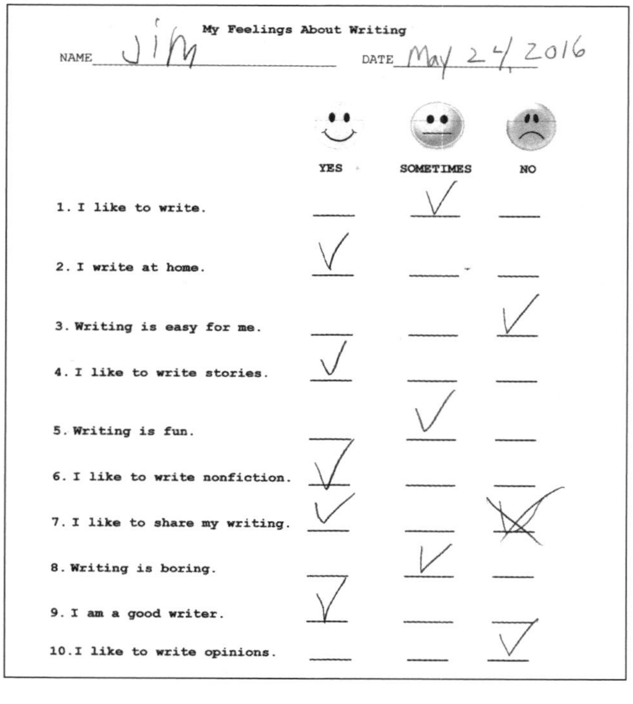
My Feelings About Writing

NAME Jim DATE May 24, 2016

	YES	SOMETIMES	NO
1. I like to write.		✓	
2. I write at home.	✓		
3. Writing is easy for me.			✓
4. I like to write stories.	✓		
5. Writing is fun.		✓	
6. I like to write nonfiction.	✓		
7. I like to share my writing.	✓		~~✓~~
8. Writing is boring.		✓	
9. I am a good writer.	✓		
10. I like to write opinions.			✓

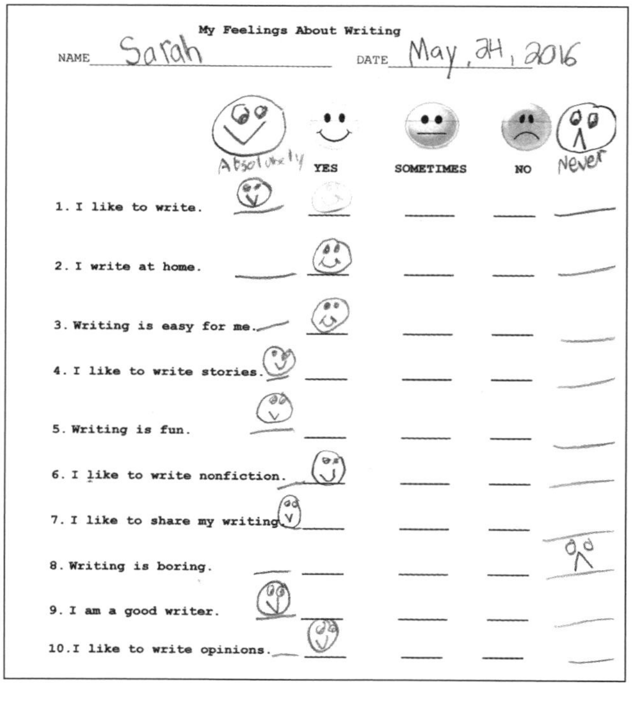
My Feelings About Writing

NAME Sarah DATE May, 24, 2016

	Absolutely	YES	SOMETIMES	NO	Never
1. I like to write.	☺				
2. I write at home.		☺			
3. Writing is easy for me.		☺			
4. I like to write stories.	☺				
5. Writing is fun.	☺				
6. I like to write nonfiction.		☺			
7. I like to share my writing.	☺				
8. Writing is boring.					☹
9. I am a good writer.	☺				
10. I like to write opinions.		☺			

In a sixth-grade end-of-quarter self-evaluation, the writers were asked to respond to the following prompts:

Think about the writing you did this quarter
- Which piece did you work hardest to write?
- What kept you going with this writing?
- Which piece do you think is your best writing this quarter?
- Why do you think it is your best?
- What did you do to revise this piece?
- How did you decide to revise it?
- What will you do to improve your writing? (What goals can you set for yourself?)

These reflections ask students to think about what they have done well, where they have expended the most effort, and how they have made decisions as writers. We end by asking students to set goals for themselves as writers, always pushing them to take risks to become better and more sophisticated writers.

Portfolios: Reflection Is Built In as Part of the Process

Formative assessment can be documented in many ways, including the creation of a working portfolio that demonstrates growth. For older students, electronic portfolios are easy to keep and add to every year. The portfolio allows reviewers to see what level of work the student achieved over time and how that student has engaged in reflective practice. Self-selected pieces show what the students are capable of at this moment in time with detailed, standards-based reflections attached to each artifact. Of course, it does require time to allow students to select their artifacts, reflect on their worth, and share these items and reflections at a teacher-student conference or a parent conference.

Portfolios could be a way to go gradeless or to support the grades in a more meaningful way. (Does a C or a 2 help us know the journey or only the final destination?) In the end, it *is* quick and easy because students take the lead. They take ownership of the assessment process and become skilled self-evaluators. They are more engaged and more invested in a process that largely involves them and gives them some choice and control. Formative assessment, such as a portfolio system, helps students become metacognitive. They understand how to represent themselves as readers, as writers, as mathematicians, and as historians. Their work shows their learning processes as well because it is work completed over time. Their entire process shows the progress they have made toward goals and standards.

Geof Hewitt in *A Portfolio Primer: Teaching, Collecting, and Assessing Student Writing* discusses student writers' "best piece" letters. The students write about why they chose the piece as best and how they composed it, adding any other comments they choose to add. "Such a letter often provides the teacher with valuable insights into the student's learning process and helps the teacher determine the extent to which the student has learned to make decisions that are independent of the teacher's judgments" (Hewitt 1995, 177). Over time, students become more prepared to discuss their writing pieces in their portfolios in meaningful ways—more prepared to take the prominent role in writing and portfolio conferences, and better prepared to continue to set new goals, both short and long term.

Self-reflection can also be represented in the tags for portfolio artifacts chosen from the working portfolio for the showcase portfolio.

- Tag your best piece. Why do you think it represents your best piece of writing?
- Tag a piece where you took a risk and tried something new. Explain what you did and how it worked for you.
- Tag your favorite/most memorable piece. Explain why you chose it.
- Tag a piece you would like to continue to revise. How would you change this piece?

Lynne kept writing portfolios in her own third- and fourth-grade classrooms because she felt selection days involved students in the assessment process, giving them opportunities for reflection, and built in celebrations with parents, siblings, grandparents, or other people who were significant in the lives of her students. Her portfolio celebrations included time to read and share, time to write notes on beautiful paper to leave for each writer, and time to make visible their growth and accomplishments as writers. Although every celebration was not the same, the two or three portfolio celebrations each year gave students a chance to share their published pieces and talk about their significance. If you'd like to try a portfolio system with your class, here are six important ideas to remember:

- Begin with a rich collection.
- Involve students in the selection process.
- Reflect (students) on artifacts chosen.
- Hold a portfolio conference during and after the selection process.
- Project. Students set long- and short-term goals independently or with the teacher.
- Celebrate! Learning should be joyful.

For elementary school students, plan a celebration, possibly when family members can come to the class and students can share their work. Lynne held one performance celebration each spring, complete with linens or tablecloths and flowers as centerpieces. She reserved the gym and asked for parents' help to organize an Authors' Tea, where students would perform a piece of writing, eat, talk, and share one reflection on this year's growth as a writer with parents, classmates, and teacher guests. Parents and guests were encouraged to browse portfolios and leave a note (special notepaper was provided) for the authors.

Goal Setting as Reflection on the Work We Do and the Work We Want to Do

When we build in opportunities for reflection, we ask students to become familiar with goal setting. Portfolio systems usually ask students to create both short- and long-term goals with a teacher or by themselves. Usually, discussion about writing goals can begin in writing workshop as whole-group discussion.

Sometimes, students will offer long-term goals that need to be divided into smaller steps. Younger students need help doing this. Kindergarteners in Kolleen Bell's class came up with seven goals, but they voted on three of them to work on for the next month. The first goal was small—adding spaces between words—an appropriate goal for kindergarteners. The second goal was more general but deals with writing fluency. Writing more sentences instead of using pictures to tell the story is an important step for these writers. Many kindergarteners in Kolleen's room were beginning to write longer pieces with three or more sentences. Some students were still focusing on the development of the picture and only writing one sentence. Developmentally, we focus first on fluency, then form, and finally correctness. Each student can be more specific here. If he is only writing one sentence, could he write one more? If she is already doing that, could she write three or four sentences about the same idea or think about expanding her story by writing a beginning, a middle, and an end?

Linked with focus lessons and modeled and shared writing experiences, a writer can evaluate his own writing to see whether he is making progress toward his goal. The last goal is tricky. Hannah explained what adding details means to her. "You can add words that describe, so color words and size words. You can explain how you feel about something. That's adding details." James elaborated: "You can add more details to the picture. You can do this before you start to write words or after that." Ryan's goal was to add more sentences. Paging through his journal, Kolleen saw that it was a good choice. Ryan had elaborate illustrations, but only one sentence on each page. He had a story about a sleepover his brother recently had. We asked him questions like, *What do you want your readers to know about the sleepover? How did everybody fit? Where did everyone sleep?* Ryan had answers for all these questions and realized he could easily add a few sentences to the page. He left the group to go to his desk and do just that. Lynne gave him a sticky note with a list of words and phrases to help him remember his words: *sleeping bags, big bedroom, watching TV.* Lynne reminded Ryan that she had not written sentences, just a list of words. Together, they read the list one time before Ryan went off to write.

James, another kindergarten student in Kolleen's class, had a conference with Lynne about his piece, "What's Sticking with Me?" (see Figure 8.4). James wrote a piece about the beach, and his goal was to add more sentences to his writing.

Lynne asked him to read it aloud two times. James noticed that he needed an s at the end of *sand castle* and added it. "Yes," Lynne told him. "You need the final s sound in words to show more than one." Lynne and James examined his drawing that showed three sand castles. "Did you build that many?" Lynne queried. James talked about building many castles over the course of a day at the beach. "It makes sense to match your words to your pictures," James said. Lynne smiled. She had heard his teacher, Kolleen, remind the students to do exactly that before they began to write in their journals. The sticky note

Figure 8.4
"What's Sticking with Me?"

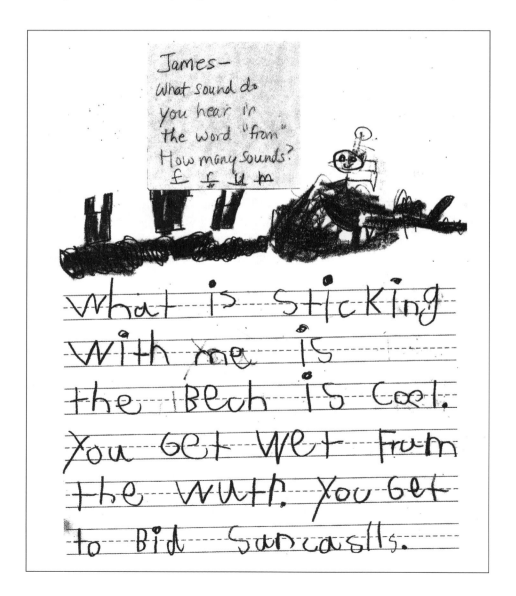

attached to the writing sample from James's notebook shows part of their conversation. Lynne capitalized on an opportunity to help James be more precise about his kid spelling. "How many sounds are in the word *from?*" Lynne asked. She helped him stretch the sounds. James realized he had forgotten an *r* and squeezed it in. Lynne did not bother to tell James that the *f* should not have been capitalized or that this word has an *o* not a *u*. She wrote a few notes to herself: *Talk with James about upper- and lowercase letters. Return to this journal entry to show James how to build content, perhaps elaborating by describing the sand castles.* Together, they looked at the goal chart (see Figure 8.5).

James felt he was meeting his goal of adding more sentences to his writing pieces. Lynne agreed. Previous pages had grown from one-sentence entries to two sentences on a page. This piece had three sentences. They counted them and noted the use of end punctuation. James wanted to move on to a new goal, adding details to his writing. Lynne readily agreed. She was sure that the beach entry would be a good place to start the next day. Lynne asked James to think about what he did to build the sand castles. James talked about using a bucket of water to make the sand so wet you could pack it. She suggested that he look at his drawing to think of another detail he could add to his writing. He said he used a plastic cup to make the turrets for his castles. Lynne nodded. "Great details, James. This could actually help someone who wants to build a sand castle." James was off to a good start to meet the next goal.

Figure 8.5
Goal-Setting Chart in Kolleen Bell's Kindergarten Class

James could use this goal through several weeks of writing. For each entry, a different plan of action could be suggested. For example, Lynne taught him to talk across five fingers as a way of adding sentences and details to his journal entries. This way, James could do some self-assessment before he came to a conference. If he could hold up five fingers while he orally rehearsed his piece aloud and again when he read his piece to himself, he probably used some details. Lynne modeled for James how to talk across her fingers with a story about her Welsh corgi. As she told her story aloud, she held up a finger at the end of each sentence. Later, she wrote the story for him as well and drew a picture that helped to display some of the details, such as the big, orange butterfly and the creek.

Merri and I went for a walk in the park. Merri started to chase after a big, orange butterfly. She stopped when the butterfly fluttered across a wide creek. Then she sat down and howled. I laughed and laughed at my funny dog!

James practiced talking across his fingers the next day with Lynne as his partner. Here is his oral rehearsal:

I like to build sand castles at the beach. I fill a bucket with some water and dump it on the sand to make it wet. I pack the sand with my fingers and shovel. Then I scoop up sand in a plastic cup to make the turrets. I made three sand castles.

Whenever possible, if a student initiates a challenge that is within his reach, it is a good idea to let him try it out. Together with the student, a plan of action can be created. Tracking a student's progress and providing feedback is essential to help a student meet his goals.

Kolleen used a page from *Don't Let the Pigeons Drive the Bus* by Mo Willems to talk about different kinds of punctuation. She projected the page onto the smart board and called on her students to count the number of sentences by noticing the end punctuation marks. As the students talked about the different end punctuation marks, Kolleen challenged them to do two things as they wrote in their journals: (1) to write your sentences and then add pictures to match the words, and (2) to think about end punctuation, adding periods, questions, and exclamation marks.

Vinny wrote about bugs, a favorite topic for him. In a conference with Kolleen, he told her that he began with a question on purpose. Kolleen asked him to read his question. Then she queried, "Vinny, what is missing at the end of your question?" Vinny's "Oh!" said it all. He wasn't sure how to make the question mark, so Kolleen drew it on a sticky note and asked Vinny to trace it several times. He added the mark during the conference. The rest of his sentences had no end punctuation. Kolleen asked him to read his piece several times and stop to point to a place that needed a period, question, or exclama-

Kolleen Bell Holds a Goal-Setting Conference with Kindergartener Vinny
http://sten.pub/ac16

tion point. (She added these marks to the sticky note on either side of the question mark.) Vinny added a period after his sentence: *Sum sting you.* He told Kolleen where he would add more end punctuation and returned to his seat to finish independently.

Kolleen made a note that she could add using end punctuation as one of Vinny's long-term goals for the rest of his kindergarten year. She felt this goal was something that students would also work on in first and second grades, too. Kolleen explained that some goals for kindergarten are short term, like drawing a picture and labeling it with words or using initial and final consonant sounds to write words. She shared that many goals depended on the individual makeup of each class. This class, for instance, was ready to try out print variation and making comparisons. The students were able to write similes, even though they did not know what they were called. Maybe Vinny could write a simile about bugs! (See Figure 8.6.)

The next day, Kolleen checked in with Vinny to see whether he had successfully added end punctuation. He had! She asked Vinny if he had met his goal of writing more sentences to accompany his drawings. Vinny counted his

Figure 8.6
Vinny's Journal Entry About Bugs

sentences—five in all. He decided he could add more details, but he wasn't sure what he had to do. Kolleen suggested that sometimes a writer just says something more about one of his details. "Can you tell me why bugs scare you?" Vinny said that he didn't like the feeling of bugs crawling on his arms and legs. "It makes me itchy," Vinny complained. "And besides, they can hurt you." Kolleen decided that some reading about bugs (even if it was mainly looking at pictures) might help Vinny to add details to his piece. Vinny was fascinated with *Bug Faces* by Darlyne Murawski. He was eager to return to his piece of writing to add more details.

Harper's conference with Kolleen clearly showed that Harper was a very competent kindergarten writer. While all students in kindergarten are not at Harper's level, we cannot hold back our writers who are ready to try craft moves and strategies beyond the level of most of their classmates. Kolleen refers to the goal-setting chart where Harper has placed her name on a sticky note next to *I will add more details to my writing*. As she shares her piece with Kolleen, her teacher praises her and then asks her to clear up some confusion about why Cam is included in this piece. As Harper explains, Kolleen suggests that she add that detail to her writing. Because Kolleen knows Harper is ready, Kolleen talks with her briefly about what many writers do to create a satisfying ending by telling what the main character is feeling. Harper is ready to do this

Harper Confers with Kolleen
Bell on Her Goal
http://sten.pub/ac17

Figure 8.7
My Writing Goal (Kolleen Bell's
Kindergarten Class)

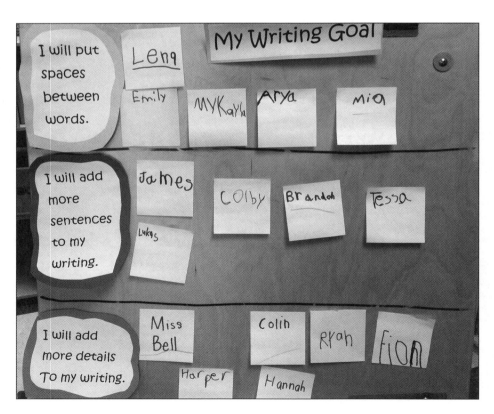

and adds while she is still sitting with Kolleen, *I would be excited if my mom got the job!* (See Figure 8.8.)

Figure 8.8
Harper's Journal Entry About Mom's Job Interview

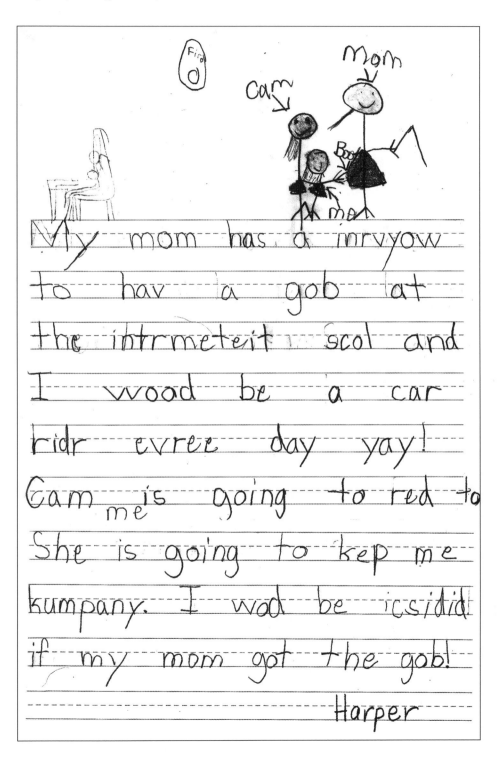

My mom has a inrvyow to hav a gob at the intrmeteit scol and I wood be a car ridr evree day yay! Cam me is going to red to She is going to kep me kumpany. I wod be icsidid if my mom got the gob!

Harper

Figure 8.9
Brandon's Conference with a
Self-Assessment Checklist:
Spacing Between Words

Figure 8.10
Brandon's Self-Assessment
Checklist

In April, Lynne held a conference with Brandon, a kindergartener in Kolleen's classroom. Lynne wanted to talk with Brandon about his attempt to use a self-assessment checklist for the last piece of writing he did in his journal. The following conversation ensued:

Lynne: So Brandon, can you explain how you used the checklist?

Brandon: After I do my work, I check these off (*pointing to the boxes on the self-assessment checklist*). I decided I am going to write all the way to the bottom. Then I will look at the checklist again. I'm not finished. (See Figure 8.9.)

Lynne: Hmm. I understand. Which part of the checklist is most helpful to you?

Brandon: Sometimes I don't use spaces. So I really need the checklist to remind me.

Lynne: So you like using the checklist.

Brandon: (*nods*) Yes. It helps me.

Lynne: What do you think you will add?

Brandon: I will add SSSSS going from the ball in my hand to the hoop.

Lynne: I think your readers will know you sank the ball and scored!

Brandon: Ms. Bell says that sometimes your picture does the talking!

Brandon and most of his classmates seemed to enjoy their new tool. While Lynne noticed that most of the kindergarteners had checked all the boxes on the checklist, she did observe some students, including Brandon, rereading their pieces, and waiting until after they were sure they had finished drafting before checking anything. Kolleen had waited until March to introduce the self-assessment, a smart move because the students were ready for it. As she always did, Kolleen asked her student writers to gather on the rug for a discussion about the checklist so she could ask her young writers to explain each item in their own words. "When do you think you should check neat handwriting?" Kolleen asked. "What does it mean to have neat handwriting?" As students commented on the different items, Kolleen sometimes added her thinking. "Okay. It is true that you use capital letters to start a sentence and for people's names, but I am also going to add that you need to look at your writing to see if you used capital letters where they do not belong." She displayed writing from last year in which a student had capitalized the letters *b* and p wherever they occurred. "Should this student check the capital letters box?" After the discussion, the students were encouraged to try out the checklist with their latest journal entry or the new one they were going to write that day. As with goal-setting conferences, Kolleen was giving her students a chance to be part of the assessment process. (See Figure 8.10.)

Our Final Thoughts

Sometimes, we can create an experience that will give all our students a chance to evaluate their writing and share their thinking with others. In Brenda Krupp's third-grade class, a whole-group conference where students had a chance to share something they felt went very well and one area that needed some help allowed students to problem-solve as a giant think tank (see Chapter 6, "Teacher and Student"). The responses were honest and sincere. Another strategy for sharing aspects of writing students are proud of is to form an inside and outside circle. Students on the inside circle sit facing the students on the outside circle. After the students have had time to share, the students on the inside circle shift to the left or right and the new partners share. Then, the teacher can shift the discussion to ask students to share a part of the writing that still needs work or a helpful suggestion.

In *Day by Day: Refining Writing Workshop Through 180 Days of Reflective Practice*, Ayres and Shubitz (2010) suggest copying both sides of a paper with a rubric so that teachers and students are using the same instrument to assess a writing piece. They also recommend a space for student comments; in other words, students support the decisions they make in self-assessment with solid reasons—basically, evidence from their text. When student writers take their time to reexamine a piece they believe to be "finished," they may start to notice the tracks of the teaching in their text. Lynne asks students to look through their writer's notebook and possibly a class binder that stores notes from mini-lessons and shared writing experiences. Perhaps there is something to add, to delete, or to move based on this review. When we give students opportunities to talk about their writing using the same tool we will use to offer praise, polish, and a grade, we create a quality culture for the drafting process. The act of self-assessment will encourage students to use the rubric (or perhaps a checklist) to revise their writing before they offer it as a final draft. If we truly believe that reflection and self-evaluation, including goal setting, is important, we will make time for it within our day—quiet time for students to think as well as write.

If we model writerly behaviors, including reflection, we demonstrate that we believe reflection is important. Metacognition, thinking about our thinking and our practices, is a way for us to grow as educators. Teachers can reflect on how students are using the craft moves and strategies introduced in the focus lessons in their pieces. They can evaluate whether the choices the students are making are helping them improve as writers. Teachers can reflect on student engagement, an important goal throughout the day. It may be a management issue that needs attention. Do you need to rethink what your students are doing while you are conferring with your students? Are students making good choices for peer conference partners? It's a good idea to ask a grade-level partner or literacy coach to observe the writing workshop for an opportunity to reflect through collaborative conversations. Sometimes, you can even ask your students for help: *Was it easy to find a good place to get your work done today?* We must remember that reflection will help all of us, not just our students.

Building in reflection isn't easy and takes a lot of practice. Growing student writers never happens instantly. It happens over time. But it isn't accidental either. It takes persistence and a boatload of patience. Don't give up if you are disappointed with students' initial attempts at reflection. As students continue to have opportunities to share their reflections, they will improve over time. Daily reflection will help them imagine the possibilities for their writing and make choices that are sensible and meaningful. Helping students develop a growth mind-set where challenges are welcomed and struggle is something to be expected will help students develop as thinkers who make sage decisions. Opportunities to make choices and engage in self-reflection are essential to grow successful writers.

Chapter 9

QUICK AND EASY
Tips to Formative Assessment That Will Help You Maintain Your Sanity in the Age of Testing

> "The shift to a growth mindset demands a corresponding shift in language to discuss the learning and assessing processes . . . When students ask about grades, challenge them to think about learning.
>
> —Starr Sackstein, *Hacking Assessment*

An essential part of educating students successfully is assessing their progress in meeting high standards. Done well and thoughtfully, assessments are tools for learning and promote progress, equity, and reflective practice. They provide important information to teachers, to their students, and to their students' families to measure progress toward achievable goals. Done without clear purpose and in excess, assessments take away valuable time from teaching and learning and remove or greatly limit everything from creativity and choice to collaboration that takes place in K–12 classrooms.

Sound assessment plays a vital role in showing and in detailing progress students are making toward reasonable goals and in helping educators monitor and adjust instruction in their classrooms. Professional development opportunities concerning formative assessment practices may help school districts do a better job of supporting teachers and principals to use it to guide decision making and to inform instructional practices. Formative assessment may not necessarily affect students' grades or determine whether they will be promoted to the next grade or placed in a special class. It will, however, help teachers know what their students are able to do and what they need to learn.

Formative assessment can significantly increase students' level of participation and engagement. Teachers' instructional practices change as they embrace new standards and new ways to assess progress efficiently and meaningfully daily. Teachers can plan and review lessons after having a clear understanding

141

of what they need to do. Formative assessment can focus on students' needs, providing instant feedback and allowing teachers to customize, or differentiate, instruction on a day-to-day basis.

Status of the Class

Nancie Atwell's seminal book *In the Middle* introduced the concept of "status of the class" (1987, 89). Status of the class is a valuable tool in helping both student writers and their teachers to set goals not only for the day but also for the unit of study. As we prepare to work with our students, we recognize where they are in the process, and they recognize that they are held accountable for the work that they do each day. Writing workshop allows for choice; however, choice does not mean that students can choose to read instead of write (unless they are reading to do research for writing or to study a mentor text to imitate a craft move) or that students can plan interminably. We cannot meet with every student every day or even every week, but taking a status of the class each day at the beginning of writing workshop is a way to keep track of progress. Through this two-minute activity, we can determine which students need our immediate attention, which students might just need a roving conference, and which students are okay working independently that day.

In Kelly Gallagher's second-grade classroom, Kelly does a quick status of the class at either the opening or the close of writing workshop. Sometimes, she even fits it in twice. Kelly says that this quick check-in helps her see where her students are, who needs help or a gentle push, and what they are accomplishing in one workshop period. In the video, you will see Kelly gather her community close to her on the rug. They bring their notebooks with them, and as Kelly calls their names, they respond quickly with some choice words or phrases that identify their place in the process of composing: planning, drafting, revising, ready to publish, need a conference. Kelly likes to use a column titled *Completed*. She explained, "I know a writer is never really finished—there's always an opportunity to do more revision and editing—but we have to have deadlines in second grade, too. When I look down the *Completed* column, I can get a sense of where most of my students are in a unit of study. So, if we are writing informational pieces, I can decide if I can begin mini-lessons on writing stories, if that is our next area to study." Sometimes, during a status of the class, Kelly will say something like, *Were you able to add those details we talked about into your piece? Okay, you're ready to publish.* A simple asterisk with the words *needs help* will signal to Kelly that she and her students may be able to help a writer who is stuck or experiencing writer's block. Kelly says it usually takes anywhere from one to three minutes for this activity, and the time spent here is well worth it. "Just the expectation of this roll call is a gentle nudge for students to spend their time in workshop each day in a productive way. They know they must be engaged to make the most of their time," Kelly explained. (See Figure 9.1.)

Status of the Class: Kelly Gallagher, Grade Two
http://sten.pub/ac18

Figure 9.1
Status of the Class Grade Two

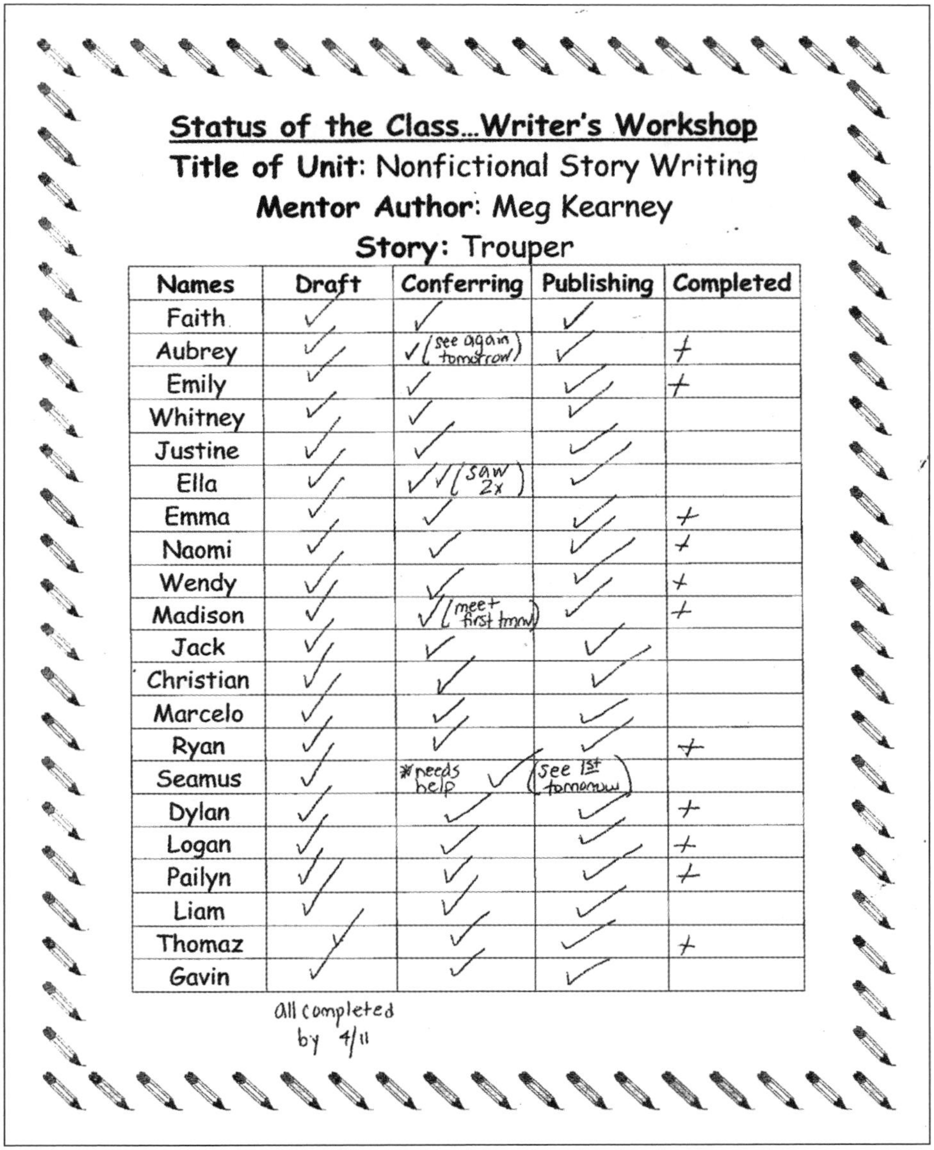

Status of the Class...Writer's Workshop
Title of Unit: Nonfictional Story Writing
Mentor Author: Meg Kearney
Story: Trouper

Names	Draft	Conferring	Publishing	Completed
Faith	✓	✓	✓	
Aubrey	✓	✓ (see again tomorrow)	✓	✝
Emily	✓	✓	✓	✝
Whitney	✓	✓	✓	
Justine	✓	✓	✓	
Ella	✓	✓✓ (saw 2x)	✓	
Emma	✓	✓	✓	✝
Naomi	✓	✓	✓	✝
Wendy	✓	✓	✓	✝
Madison	✓	✓ (meet first tmrw)	✓	✝
Jack	✓	✓	✓	
Christian	✓	✓	✓	
Marcelo	✓	✓	✓	
Ryan	✓			✝
Seamus	✓	*needs help ✓	see 1st tomorrow	
Dylan	✓		✓	✝
Logan	✓	✓	✓	✝
Pailyn	✓	✓	✓	✝
Liam	✓	✓		
Thomaz	✓	✓	✓	✝
Gavin		✓	✓	

All completed by 4/11

Knowing where your student writers are in the process is an important formative assessment tool. If a student has been drafting for several days without moving forward, we need to know why. Is it because the writer is stuck? Or is the writer doing some deep thinking or research? Conferring with this student will clear this up. Keeping the status of the class alerts the teacher to the need for a conference. The following status of the class was used during an informational writing unit of study in one sixth-grade classroom. It uses the following codes: P = Prewrite, R = Research, D = Draft, V = Revise, and PR = Peer review. Ab indicates the student was absent that day. A quick review of the status indicates that most students are drafting or researching; a few have done some revision; and a few also have met with a peer for reviewing what

Figure 9.2
Status of the Class Grade Six

they have drafted. A concern is that during the five days recorded in this status most students continue to draft. Does that mean these students are doing no revising? Probably not, but it's important for the teacher to find out and to nudge the writers to move forward in their pieces. Notice Alexia who has used five days for prewriting. Alexia needs a conference. Is her problem that the topic is too broad? Is it that she is having difficulty with organization? Is she changing topics? Five days is too long a time to spend on prewriting! (See Figure 9.2.)

Overall, Diane and Lynne agree that the status-of-the-class checklist is a quick, routine check-in with each student on a daily basis. It can begin or end a writing workshop, but its regular use will establish a routine that slightly raises the level of concern to ensure productivity, and, even more important, it gives you an easy way to connect with every student each day. What a great opportunity to formatively assess at the same time. Teachers can adapt it to fit their needs and the needs of the students in their classroom. Together, with your students, you can make a chart of the kinds of responses that fit these needs.

Helpful Lists

One of the most frustrating things in a writing classroom is to hear groans and moans of "I don't have anything to write about" from your students. Nip this problem in the bud before it blossoms into a larger one. Take care of it at the beginning of the year. Writer's block can be overcome. It is not an excuse to avoid writing for the entire school year! During the first month or two, observe and keep a list of students who always seem to be stuck or just do not know how to come up with a topic. Then, use an interest survey or one-on-one interview (keep it short) to learn about those students. Tempt them with a writing territories list, expert list, a heart or hand map, a neighborhood map, or memory chains. Lists of happy times, sad times, pet peeves, and embarrassing moments can also provide topic ideas. Look at the student writing you have, whatever it may be, and list the strategies the student is using and ones that he may be ready to use or need to use in the near future.

Conference Clocks

A quick and easy way to manage conferences is to provide students with a conference clock and ask students to take three minutes to make appointments with one, two, or three peers. Usually, some method must be employed to do this efficiently. Teachers sometimes set timers or play music and then give a one-minute warning. Lynne encouraged her students to find different partners as the year progressed. Students soon found out on their own that classmates they may not have initially chosen for a conference provided them with good suggestions. When a student makes an appointment with a peer, that classmate must also write the student who is making the appointment in the same time slot on his own conference sheet. In the beginning, Lynne suggested eight minutes for a rotation, giving approximately four minutes for each person in the pair. Later, she reduced the time to six minutes. Students offered a praise and a push, copying the "push" onto a sticky note for their partner. These were placed in the quadrant of the conference clock that corresponded to the appointment of the responder. Then writers could decide on their own what suggestions they'd like to use. (See Figure 9.3; also available online at sten. pub/acloserlook.)

Figure 9.3
Conference Clock

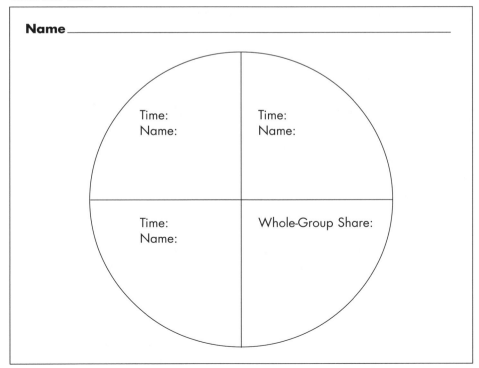

Blogs

In today's classrooms, technology offers us quick ways to assess student learning. Students can respond to a space on a class blog that is dedicated for this purpose. A teacher can decide how often a student must post a reflection about his work. We suggest no more than once a week. Because the posts can be viewed by both the teacher and the students, it will be easy to track growth. In addition, when students read the self-reflection of their peers, it may provide insight into the review process without any coaching from the teacher. Sackstein proposes *Kidblog* as a platform for younger students and *Blogger* for older ones (Sackstein 2015b). She suggests that blogs like these will help to develop digital citizenship skills by giving students repeated opportunities to consider the reflective thinking of their peers, as well as their own reflections. Sackstein asserts, "The additional perspective of an audience and the power of connection can only enhance this learning in a new dimension" (Sackstein 2015b, 36). We agree and have found that blogs not only create an online community of writers and readers but also maintain that community. Mary Buckelew, director of the Pennsylvania Writing and Literature Project, asks her undergraduate and graduate students to read teacher posts on *write.share. connect* (https://pawlpblog.org/) and to respond to a few that speak to them. Teachers also comment that starting a classroom blog helps students grow their identities as writers and readers. In a whole-group discussion, the graduate students overwhelmingly agreed that if their students had an opportunity to post their writing on a blog and get instant readership and some feedback from their peers and possibly their teacher, they would most likely write more and be more likely to engage in revision.

Tweets

Pose a reflection question on the whiteboard and challenge your students to respond to it in 140 characters or less. For older students, using the Socrative Student app is one way to respond to formative assessment questions in a variety of formats, including an exit slip. Once students launch the Socrative Student app, they'll be prompted to join the teacher's room via the teacher's unique code. No student accounts are necessary to use this app. Of course, a classroom blog site could have a page for tweets or a special form could be made for students to compose their tweets and share with their partner or peer response group, or teachers can collect the tweets to take notes on how students handle the reflection question that was posed. Some example questions follow:

- What worked well for you today?
- What new goal can you set for yourself based on the work you accomplished here?

- What is one important thing you learned about opinion writing?
- Did you make good choices during your writing time today? Explain.

Exit Slips

Quick formative assessment tools are admit and exit slips. Asking students to reflect and respond to an end-of-the-class question, such as *What do you now know about informational writing?* can inform our instruction. Exit slips take only a few minutes to read but tell us a great deal. In a fourth-grade classroom, Ms. Karen Drew's students shared their exit slips at the beginning of the next writing workshop as an admit slip. They shared their exit slips in small groups and tried to reach consensus about this type of writing. Their conversations and responses in whole-group share to create an anchor chart showed their learning. Karen and Lynne were able to look at the responses and know that these fourth graders had a solid understanding of how to write an informational piece. However, they also talked about what was missing. Not one student had talked about organizational structures (except for description) to frame informative writing, such as compare and contrast, cause and effect, or problem and solution, or the use of transitional words and phrases to move a reader through the text. That would be fodder for new focus lessons and a lens to use to reexamine students' writing.

As they studied the charted responses and returned to the exit slips, Lynne and Karen had an aha moment. No one talked about audience: *What type of audience are you writing for?* A mini-lesson on purpose and audience would fit nicely into the next week of writing workshop, too. Karen also wondered whether she needed to do a lesson on writing in the real world where genres are mixed. She started to hunt for real-world examples of informational/narrative or informational/opinion writing. She debated whether her fourth graders would understand global structures and substructures in a piece of writing. This is a necessary part of formative assessment. As teachers, we start to question what our writers need at this moment in time and how valuable it will be. Here are the fourth graders' collective thoughts about informational writing:

- It explains something that most readers do not know about.
- Informational writing needs facts, not fiction.
- Sometimes you need statistics and quotes to support your big ideas.
- An anecdote is a little story you can use in informational writing so you don't always use main ideas and details all the time.
- It adds to information of the readers and sometimes provides options.
- Informational writing gives new information to the readers. It's not about writing what everybody already knows.
- Your writing can include the latest research on the topic.
- It can be tricky. Writers that write informational texts sometimes include their opinions.
- It describes a person, a place, or an event in history.

Admit Slips

Admit slips, too, can be used as formative assessment. Sometimes admit slips are given as a homework assignment collected as the students file into the classroom. In general, these slips may be a response to an assigned reading. This is an ideal time to let students write deep (not surface) questions about their reading; questions that can be answered by reading exactly what the author wrote would not be acceptable for an admit slip question. Scaffold question starters to help students begin to formulate questions about their reading, for example, *Why did . . . ? How did . . . ? What caused . . . ?* Student questions can be read aloud (without using student names) at the start of class and can become the basis for discussion. Teachers can learn a great deal about their student readers and writers from the admit slip as well. What kinds of questions are students asking? Which types of questions produce more spirited discussion and debate? Do students delve deeply into the text, or are they still skimming the surface?

As with exit slips, admit slips are ungraded. Ungraded does not mean unevaluated, however. Admit slips show the teacher what students are able to do, and they help teachers to plan focus lessons and to group students for instruction. Teachers may use these slips as a kind of self-assessment: what lessons have stuck, what lessons need to be repeated, what lessons need to be tweaked, and what lessons should be redone from scratch.

SPOTLIGHT ON FORMATIVE ASSESSMENT

When a Child Talks . . . We Learn

Who does conferring belong to in my classroom? Many images of conferring show teachers sitting in chairs or kneeling alongside of students. The teacher asks the questions and the student does the talking. In theory, conferring belongs to both student and teacher. The student learns by talking. How do we ensure that the experience, results, and impact of the conference remain with the teacher and student beyond that single moment?

Writing as the teacher, I realize record keeping matters. Yet, it can be challenging. I've tried many variations of coding and shorthand. In the process of conferring and recording by hand, I find myself distracted and not fully absorbing what the student says. Additionally, my ability to engage the art of conversation—listening and asking questions to nudge the speaker further into his or her thoughts—suffers. In the end, my hand-scrawled notes serve as nice evidence of conferring, but they do not necessarily help me help the student.

I'm struck by something specific that Donald Murray wrote: "I must listen and the students must do the talking" (2009, 70). If Murray meant "listen and write" he would have written *listen and write*. But he did not. He wrote *listen*. Yet, I have often felt obligated to scribble hieroglyphics onto yellow legal pads while students poured out their thoughts, struggles, triumphs, and discoveries. I wonder what opportunities for growth we may have missed.

I have read that students should write four times more than a teacher could possibly read or respond to—could the same be true of conferring? Should students be conferring four times more than a teacher could ever participate in? I imagine this depends on to whom we feel the conferring belongs.

Currently, I use the app Voice Record Pro to record conferences because it works on my iPhone. I use it, too, because I am able to easily store and manage conferences in a variety of places: e-mail or SMS, Google Drive, Dropbox, OneDrive, Box, or SoundCloud. However, I immediately upload the conferences to a private unlisted YouTube channel. By keeping records in this manner, I am able to place my device down on the desk and truly engage in listening to the student writer. I am also able to share conferences with the students, parents, administration, or guidance counselors if need be.

However, I am back to my original question: Who does conferring belong to in my classroom? Do I still wield more ownership than there needs to be, even if the student is doing the bulk of the talking? One way I am going to examine and reflect on these questions is by inviting my students to record their own conferences with their writing partners. My classroom is a BYOD classroom and most students bring in a personal device. For those who do not, I have a classroom set of iPads and Chromebooks. My students sit with self-selected writing partners. We write four out of the five days in class, and the writing partners discuss and share throughout the entire process when they feel they need it.

I am wondering how Murray would feel about the possibility of students recording their own student-to-student conferring sessions and then uploading selected conferences (student choice) to a classroom YouTube channel or a shared classroom folder in Google Drive or Dropbox. I imagine we may be crossing into a new and relatively unexplored territory of ownership and access. Imagine building a library of student-to-student and teacher-to-student conferences where all students have the ability to listen and learn from each other—beyond their writing partners, beyond the one-on-one with me, and beyond the confinement of time and space in school. My current classroom research has led me to experiment with the creation of just such a library.

After all, some students already set up shared documents—on their own—or e-mail stories to friends for feedback. The more I set my yellow legal pads down, and the more I simply listen, I hear the students tell me that they want feedback . . . they want conversation . . . they want to share . . . and they want it with their peers. They want to own the conferring process because it is deeper with a friend than with a teacher. Deeper might just mean more meaningful. Why wouldn't I (or we) create the space and conditions for those deeper, more meaningful, connections and discoveries? I have been recording conferences in which students share just how much—how deeply and specifically—they discuss writing without me. This is powerful and instructive for me to hear. In their own way, students have been telling me who the conferring should belong to in this classroom. I am wondering whether my students are speaking to you as well?

Reference

Murray, Donald. 2017. *The Essential Don Murray: Lessons from America's Greatest Writing Teacher*, ed. Thomas Newkirk and Lisa C. Miller. Portsmouth, NH: Heinemann.

Brian Kelley, M.Ed., is a codirector of the Pennsylvania Writing and Literature Project and a middle school teacher in the Unionville-Chadds Ford School District.

Leader or Learner

Sometimes, through simple charting, we can assess where our students are on their journey toward understanding a complex concept, a craft move, a writing type or form, or a process. From this chart, we can take away many things about our student writers. Are they knowledgeable and confident enough to teach or demonstrate a concept, move, or process to a peer? Are they independent thinkers? Are they risk takers? Can they take the lead, or are they, at this moment in time, only ready to follow? Are they at a place of balance—willing to lead about half of the time, while understanding they sometimes need to be the learner? Can they offer their reflections about their choices and talk about a place or two where they are almost ready to transition to a leader position? In *Hacking Assessment: 10 Ways to Go Gradeless in a Traditional Grades School*, Starr Sackstein (2015a) suggests a leader/learner chart as a way to assess progress and perhaps form efficient peer writing groups. In Karen Rhoads's fourth-grade classroom, Lynne and Karen used this chart to do exactly that— form effective peer response groups for the narrative writing unit. Here are the categories:

- Can explain many ways to find a topic to write about
- Knows what to eliminate to keep a piece focused
- Knows what a lead paragraph needs
- Can demonstrate how to show instead of tell
- Has strategies for developing the plot
- Can demonstrate how to use a splash of dialogue
- Makes use of transitional words and phrases to help the reader move through a sequence of events
- Can write a satisfying ending with a combination of strategies
- Has editing strategies

Karen asked her students to place their sticky note in one column for each category: (1) *Learner*—someone who is still developing the strategy or needs some coaching, a metacognitive conversation, or another shared/guided writing experience to feel confident and achieve proficiency; or (2) *Leader*—someone who could act as a coach or feels confident about this strategy, element of narrative writing, or area. (See Figure 9.4.)

Figure 9.4
Mrs. Karen Rhoads's Learner or
Leader Chart

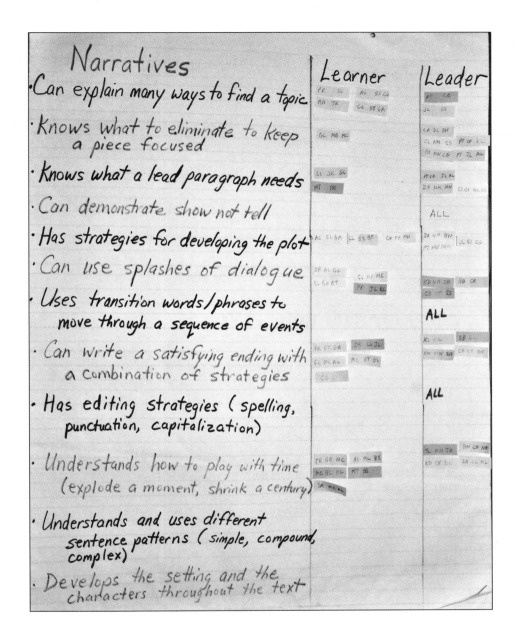

3-2-1

Here, students can respond to prompts to help them reflect: *Write about three things you tried today, two questions or wonderings you still have, and one thing you will try in the next writing workshop.* Another possibility for reflection could include: *Write about three things that went well in your workshop time today, two choices you made during your writing time that helped you move forward, and one problem that you solved or that remains unsolved. Talk about the strategies you tried or the ones you may try tomorrow.* Other variations include:

3 things you discovered

2 interesting sentences in your writing or a peer's writing

1 question you might have

3 key words

2 new writing topics, formats, or strategies

1 thought to think about

3 differences between _____ and _____

2 effects of _____ on _____

1 insight about yourself as a learner

Thumbs Up, Thumbs Down

For younger students, this is a quick assessment a teacher can use at various points in the mini-lesson to check for understanding. This practice can be used to determine which students need additional instruction in small, flexible groups or one-on-one. Some teachers add a thumb to the side or a wave of the hand to indicate that there is uncertainty or confusion. Students can use this strategy during writerly conversations to note agreement or disagreement with big ideas. Designated hand signals can help you get a picture of your students' understandings of a certain concept, strategy, or process. Using American sign language can add a new dimension to student engagement for all of your students, especially English learners.

Fact/Values List

When you begin a new unit of study, ask students to write down everything they know to be true about the topic/type of writing/craft move in the left-hand column and everything they believe to be true in the right-hand column. This will create immediate engagement with the topic and give you a sense of prior knowledge and interest. This list also could reveal misconceptions and gaps in background knowledge.

Use Conferences to Differentiate Instruction

One of the most effective uses of teacher time is to know what mini-lessons are going to be used for whole-class instruction and which ones can be taught in small-group and one-on-one conferences. In September, it is important to get your students writing every day—small pieces, poems, descriptions, commentary, observations, as well as stories, opinion pieces, and informational texts. But don't grade most of it. Just use this rich collection to help you know what your students know and what they need to know to grow and become more sophisticated. Then, select mini-lessons that will benefit these students, and group the students according to their needs for instruction in small-group conferences. Remember that most strategies work across genres with a little tweaking.

Quick-Writes

Ask students to respond to a prompt or an open-ended question before the mini-lesson, during the instruction, or after the independent writing period. Allow them two to five minutes to respond. This formative assessment can say much about how writers can think on their feet and problem-solve, use their grammar and conventions knowledge, and create a cohesive piece that has a logical, meaningful order.

Reflective Journals: Student Data Notebooks

Students keep a notebook to track their progress. They can write about where they are right now as writers and where they are headed. This notebook can discuss goals and the progress toward goals, detailing plans or steps taken to meet those goals. Collect and review them, possibly looking at six to eight notebooks per week, or ask students to bring them to a one-on-one conference or a small-group conference.

Debriefing is another form of reflection that is particularly useful in writing workshop. After presenting student writers with a strategy or craft move, give them a statement (or two) to reflect on as they practice using the craft move. For example, if the lesson focuses on expanding sentences for sentence fluency (combining sentences or parts of sentences to add details), you might ask students to reflect on the following questions: *What did you learn about using conjunctions?* or *What do you now know about combining sentences?* or *Where can you use this craft move again in your writing?* During sharing time, ask students to respond to the question by talking to a partner or in whole group. Giving students time to reflect on what they know and how they know it is great formative assessment. It allows the teacher to listen in on student thinking and to make necessary changes in instruction when necessary.

Index Cards Summaries/Questions

Three or four times a year, hand out index cards and ask students to use both sides of the card to list a big idea that they understand from the present unit of study and to write a summary statement about that big idea. Next, ask students to identify something (a strategy, a craft move, a concept) about the unit that they do not yet fully understand or have a question about and write about it as a statement or question. These cards can help you easily identify strategies and processes you may need to revisit and reteach, or the cards can signal full steam ahead!

Think-Pair-Share/Think-Ink-Pair-Share

To review craft lessons or as a way to assess student understanding of a writing strategy, ask students to write about what they know about using the strategy. Students form their responses (we like to have them write their statements in ink in their notebooks) and then share their thinking with a partner. You can call on several pairs to share their thinking. After they share, students can return to their written response to revise their thinking if necessary. As formative assessment, you can determine which students need further instruction.

Write Me a Letter

In upper grades, we like to ask students to communicate by writing letters expressing their questions, concerns, and ideas in a nonthreatening way. Keep a "mailbox" available for students to post their correspondence to you. They can write suggestions, questions, or concerns about writing workshop. We can learn a great deal about our students and from our students when we keep the lines of communication open and when students feel free to communicate honestly. If you are concerned about the time it may take you to respond to these letters, you can always limit the use of the mailbox to one day per week or several days each month, or just try it out for one marking period.

Freewriting

For fluency and to uncover their thinking about a topic (especially important in genres like informative and opinion/argument), allow students to write nonstop on a particular subject for a limited time. Freewrites are stream-of-consciousness pieces that let students discover what they already know about a particular topic, what they think about a topic, and how they might design a written piece about that topic. Even in primary grades, freewriting can be valuable, showing student writers that they do have something to say without worrying too much about getting it "right." This kind of writing gives us a picture of students' writing fluency and their agility of mind—how they can think on their feet.

Our Final Thoughts

The students in our classrooms are on a continuum and are constantly moving on that continuum. If we teach students to understand the standards and track their own progress, we are providing a lifetime of opportunities. Building reflection time into all learning helps both students and teachers. Teaching students to reflect on what they know based on the standards and their use of evidence from their writer's notebooks, portfolios, anchor charts, and class discussions to back it up will help teachers understand where their students are and where they need to go next. We must remember that learning is a reciprocal experience. We can begin to change the way we use assessment in our classrooms by understanding formative assessment, not only to drive instruction in our writing workshop but also to energize the talk in parent-teacher and student-teacher conferences, in professional development sessions, and in state departments of education. Human beings are, by nature, gregarious creatures who work best in collaborative environments.

1

AFTERWORD

"If we expand our definition and consider how we use it [assessment] to our advantage, we don't have to breathlessly await state test results in hopes that our students showed growth. We can take matters into our own hands if we are willing to include and use what we see and hear in our classrooms every day as data.

—Cris Tovani, *So What Do They Really Know?*

Internalizing the Process: Helping a Student with Self-Reflection

Rushing is the word that comes to mind when we watch Jared during writing workshop. He takes his paper and sketches his story across four pages in three minutes. Once his story is planned, he composes it in less than seven minutes. Then he is off to begin his next piece.

Jared produces lots of writing and many stories, but when he tries to reread his story to a writing partner he can't read his own writing. He lowers his head into his hands and releases an exasperated sigh of frustration. This continues to happen day after day. Setting a goal to "slow down" or "take his time" doesn't seem to have much impact. He knows his goal, but it doesn't change his behavior.

So how do we help Jared slow down? What strategies will help him utilize his skills when he is writing independently? What does he understand about his own writing process?

We decide to confer with Jared.

Teacher: What do you do well as a writer?

Jared: Wait . . . What do I . . .?

Teacher: What do you do well as a writer? What are you good at?

Jared: [Looks at his paper.] Leads. I used dialogue.

Teacher: Yes, you did. It is important to know what you do well so you can continue doing it. What do you think you need to learn as a writer?

Jared: I know! I know! I need to slow down and spell better.

Teacher: Wow! You also know what you are learning. Good for you. You can't get better at your goal if you don't know it. So, how do you slow down? How do you make sure you are using your spelling strategies?

Jared: [Shrugs.]

Now we understand a bit more about Jared. He knows what he needs to learn but doesn't know how to execute it. Since Jared is frustrated by not being able to read his own writing, we decide to show him ways to slow down and improve his spelling.

Teacher: When you are learning something new, it helps to have steps. The steps show you how to meet your goal. Let's think what we do when we try to spell a word we do not know.

Jared: You mean like what do I do to figure out how to spell it?

Teacher: Exactly. What do you do first, second, etc.?

We identify each step and write it on a sticky note:

Then we quickly model how to use it to scaffold remembering the steps to figure out how to spell a word we don't know. Our modeling is heavy-handed the first week:

Teacher: Point to the step you are on. Good. Do you know what to do?

Jared: Yes.

Teacher: Okay, do the step. Now go on to step two.

The next week Jared shows a bit of independence, and we watch from a distance. Each time he reverts to old habits, we give a nonverbal signal that redirects him to point to the steps. As the days progress, so does Jared.

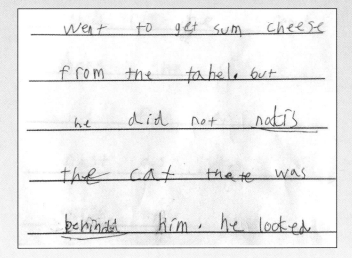

Teacher: What do you notice about your writing?

Jared: [A huge smile spread across his face.] I can read my writing! I think you can too!

We know Jared will need this series of lessons again and again throughout the school year, but the more he internalizes these steps the more his work will reflect what he knows as a reader and as a writer. Jared now knows it is not enough to know your goal; you also need to know the steps to reach your goal.

Clare Landrigan and **Tammy Mulligan**, coauthors of *Assessment in Perspective: Focusing on the Reader Behind the Numbers* (Stenhouse, 2013), have been working as a team for the past eighteen years. They began their work together coteaching an integrated first- and second-grade classroom at the Eliot Pearson Children's School in Medford, Massachusetts. Clare and Tammy now run a private staff development business, Teachers to Teachers. They work with varied school systems to implement best practices in the field of literacy and to engage in institutional change.

Teacher expertise does matter! Sharing ideas with colleagues, attending conferences, and reading professional books and blogs, such as https://twowritingteachers and https://pawlpblog.org, the blog of the Pennsylvania Writing and Literature Project, as well as assessmentinperspective.com, can be helpful. A packaged program may add a dimension, but nothing can substitute for everyday conferences and the time we set aside so that everyone is writing. In our writing workshop, it is important to value process, the journey, as much as we value product, the destination. Although our time is limited, there are several professional books that are classics for writing workshop and include valuable information about writing workshop, conferring, and feedback (this list is also available online at sten.pub/acloserlook):

Anderson, Carl. 2005. *Assessing Writers*. Portsmouth, NH: Heinemann.

Atwell, Nancie. 2015. *In the Middle: A Lifetime of Learning About Writing, Reading, and Adolescents*. 3rd ed. Portsmouth, NH: Heinemann.

Calkins, Lucy. 1994. *The Art of Teaching Writing*. Portsmouth, NH: Heinemann.

Fletcher, Ralph. 2001. *Writing Workshop: The Essential Guide*. Portsmouth, NH: Heinemann.

Glover, Matt. 2009. *Engaging Young Writers, Preschool–Grade 1*. Portsmouth, NH: Heinemann.

Johnston, Peter. 2004. *Choice Words: How Our Language Affects Children's Learning*. Portland, ME: Stenhouse.

———. 2012. *Opening Minds: Using Language to Change Lives*. Portland, ME: Stenhouse.

Overmeyer, Mark. 2009. *What Student Writing Teaches Us: Formative Assessment in the Writing Workshop*. Portland, ME: Stenhouse.

———. 2015. *Let's Talk: Managing One-on-One, Peer, and Small-Group Conferences*. Portland, ME: Stenhouse.

Pryle, Marilyn. 2009. *Purposeful Conferences, Powerful Writing! Strategies, Tips, and Teacher-Student Dialogues for Helping Kids Improve Their Writing*. New York: Scholastic Teaching Resources.

Ray, Katie Wood. 2004. *About the Authors: Writing Workshop with Our Youngest Writers*. Portsmouth, NH: Heinemann.

Routman, Regie. 2004. *Writing Essentials: Raising Expectations and Results While Simplifying Teaching*. Portsmouth, NH: Heinemann.

Even though we may have to give standardized tests, we are in charge of our own classroom. What we value can be reflected in the way that we handle assessment. It is a good idea to spend some time reflecting on this—perhaps by making a list of the ways you are currently evaluating your students' writing, what methods are most effective for you and your students, and then add to the list what you might do differently after reading this book. Lynne's list includes the following:

- Status of the class
- Ongoing anecdotal records (on sticky notes from clipboard cruising in roving conferences, targeting about six to ten students in a class period)
- Linking *Your Turn* lessons (the focus lesson) with noticings from students' writing (are they applying the craft move, using punctuation in a new way, or using the organizational scaffold?)
- Conference notes (two columns as a teacher—*What did I see the writer(s) do and hear the writer(s) say? What did I think and feel about my noticings?* Students bring their writer's notebook to conferences, too.)
- Anchor charts with students' thinking from writerly discussions (for example, noting prior grammar knowledge and recall from a discussion about a mentor passage or record each student's name next to her comment or observation)
- Spandel's six traits rubrics (revising a rubric to meet your needs and the needs of your students)
- Common Core State Standards

Take some time to reflect on what you value and believe in about how assessment can be used to help students be more successful. Make a list and share with trusted colleagues. Talk about how methods for record keeping help you see your student writers more clearly, how they prepare you for parent conferences, and how the information you gather can be shared with the individual students and drive your instruction. Formative assessment in writing workshop could be an area to focus on for your own improvement plan. A rich collection of student artifacts, audiotapes and videotapes of student conferences, and anecdotal records may become an important part of your teacher evaluation.

If you are reading this book and you are new to the profession, we hope the writing here can guide you to make and record valuable observations every day. The key to useful formative assessment is in writing your observations down and spending some time at the end of each week reflecting on these observations. You can use the information to make decisions about how your daily observations, conferences, and checklists inform your instruction. It is hard to say to another teacher, administrator, or parent, *Your child's strengths are . . . and here are a few areas of improvement. . .* when you have no artifacts or written observations to support your thinking. When students produce writing pieces, write in their notebooks, or reflect on their progress toward a goal, take a few minutes to jot down your thinking.

Of course, you will have to find a system that works best for you. The easiest and most essential record keeping is probably the daily status of the class sheet (see Chapter 9, "Quick and Easy"). Here you will record each student's progress in daily writing workshop. A glance at the status of the class sheet can provide lots of information about what each student is doing daily. In addition, you may keep a notebook with a page designated for each student, for example, attaching sticky notes from roving and one-on-one conferences (see Chapter 6, "Teacher and Student"). With these notes, it is easy to fashion small or flexible groups for highly focused instructions.

Set aside time to reflect on the records you are keeping. When Lynne served as a literacy coach for the Upper Moreland Intermediate School, she used Friday afternoons to take about two hours to review conference notes, anecdotal records, or video clips of classrooms and peer conferences. Because Diane taught four sections of writing students, she made a point to review records daily before she left school for the day, making decisions about the upcoming days and weeks.

As an example, on December 9, 2015, from notes Diane jotted down during roving conferences on narratives, she noticed that Dylan, Mike, Natalie, and Samantha were using dialogue, but they didn't have a handle on punctuating quotation marks. Because dialogue in a narrative is a good way to add detail, Diane planned for the next day's mini-lesson: *Punctuating dialogue*. Sometimes, conference notes lead to forming flexible groups: narrowing topics, for instance. The important thing is to give yourself time to use the notes you are making daily. You don't have to select Friday as your day, or the afternoon slot, but if you establish a routine for this kind of review, it will become an effective habit and make your life a lot easier when report card time rolls around.

Involve your students in this process by grooming them to articulate their own writing goals, as well as their progress toward those goals. Students must become reflective participants in their educational process. In writing workshop, they need myriad opportunities to discuss their growth and their challenges. Students must be able to see themselves as real writers, not just students who are writing for a teacher and a grade. When they learn to self-assess, they understand that writers are creators first, but later in the process, they become readers (of their own writing) and must critique honestly and fairly. They also learn that a writer is never really "finished." He just has to meet a deadline. It's great to save some edited pieces that students have published and return to them a few weeks or months later. Ask your students to offer reflections again with fresh eyes and with new knowledge. Or ask a student to examine her working portfolio midyear and at the end of the year (see Chapter 8, "Self-Assessment") and to share with you what she has discovered about herself as a writer. This conversation is always amazing, but be sure to let your student take the lead.

To help students grow, we give them feedback to encourage them to take responsible risks, to revise, and to edit their writing. There is no "correct" writing process or only one way to approach a topic and write about it. If we are to focus on a growth mind-set, we must encourage our students to see themselves as lifelong learners. And, if we truly want our students to be lifelong learners, we must be lifelong learners, too. Unlike a formal A, B, C, or points grading system, formative assessment is always a dialogue between the student and the teacher. The most significant impact on the way our students view themselves and their writing comes from the following: the oral and written feedback exchange on checklists, surveys, and rubrics; conferences and classroom discussions; discussions we document on anchor charts to make our community thinking visible and permanent. We hope that you are a teacher of writers who writes because writing workshop relies heavily on conferring and feedback. Therefore, write as often as you can. As you solve problems in your writing, it prepares you to help your students become effective problem solvers with their writing. Try keeping a writer's notebook, and write in it at least three times a week. You will grow in confidence, and if you share some of your writing with your students, they will see you as a fellow writer and not just their writing teacher.

The list of questions here is for both you and your students. These questions can be used during any kind of writing conference (not all at once!) or one or two questions can be posted on the board, chart, or website every day. Writers will get into a routine of the expectation to reflect daily—a few sentences or graphic organizer in the writer's notebook, exit or admit slip—and then a share with a partner, a response group, or the whole group before the close of workshop time. These kinds of questions ensure that students are involved in the assessment process and that it is a continuing conversation, not a teacher's one-sided monologue.

Growth Mind-Set Questions for Writing Workshop

1. What writing project have you put a lot of thought and time into in the last several weeks?
2. What did you do today as a writer that made you think hard?
3. How did you problem-solve? Did you do this alone? With a peer or peers? With the teacher? Through research and further reading?
4. What happened while you were drafting, revising, or conferring that made you want to persevere and continue to work on that piece? What aha moment or new learning emerged from this?
5. What mistake did you make that taught you something?
6. What craft move will you try next? Where?
7. What will you do to challenge yourself as a writer in the piece you are currently working on or in the next piece of writing you will start?
8. What will you do to move forward as a writer? How can you improve your writerly life?
9. What did you learn about yourself as a writer this week?
10. What effects might your writing have on your target audience, family members, classmates, community, or the world in which you live?

Above all else, we must remain flexible and patient. Giving effective feedback is a skill that comes with practice. It can always be adapted to fit the needs of a particular group of students. There are many things to consider, including the type of writing, the author's purpose and target audience, and the needs of each individual writer. Feedback is often closely linked with the goal or learning target, the individual assignment, and the individual writer. Effective feedback is descriptive in nature, specific, concise, and easy to understand. Effective feedback is motivating and empowering and, therefore, engaging. Students can use the feedback they receive to take risks and try new craft moves, conventions, and organizational structures to grow and change as writers.

Take one unit of study and try out some of the suggestions in this book—perhaps a daily status of the class, creating an interest survey or an inventory, using the roving conference, developing the conferring abilities of your students with peer conferences, and creating goals with your students with goal-setting conferences to evaluate progress toward a goal. We suggest you visit www.stenhouse.com and sign up for the Stenhouse newsletter. We hope you will look at the reference page and find other professional books and articles to explore to continue your own journey in effectively and efficiently using formative assessment to move your student writers forward.

APPENDIXES

Appendix 1   Conference Schedule for the Week of _____

Monday

Name	Comment(s)

Tuesday

Name	Comment(s)

Wednesday

Name	Comment(s)

Thursday

Name	Comment(s)

Friday

Name	Comment(s)

Appendix 2 **Conference Notes for Narrative Writing**

Name _____ **Date** _____

Interesting opening that hooks the reader and creates tension.

Satisfying ending.

Logical and appropriate organization.

The writing is about one thing.

There is variety in sentence structure and word choice.

It is easy to read and the reader doesn't stumble over the sentences as she or he reads.

The writing sounds like a person wrote it, not a robot.

Comments—strengths and/or weaknesses (grades 3–6 students write thoughts on sticky notes for immediate application).

A Closer Look: Learning More About Our Writers with Formative Assessment, K–6 by Lynne R. Dorfman and Diane Dougherty. © 2017. Stenhouse Publishers.

Appendix 3 Conference Notes for Informational Writing

Name _____ **Date** _____

Introduction to hook the reader and state the topic and purpose clearly.

Satisfying conclusion restating the big idea and the point.

Logical and meaningful organization with transitional words and phrases.

The writing is about one topic or big idea and highly focused.

Supports with relevant facts, details, definitions, explanations, examples, statistics, and quotes from experts.

There is variety in sentence structure, and word choice is precise, often using domain-specific vocabulary.

The writing sounds like a person wrote it, not a robot.

Comments—strengths and/or weaknesses (grades 3–6 students write comments on sticky notes for immediate application).

Appendix 4 Conference Notes for Opinion Writing

Name _____   **Date** _____

Introduction clearly states the opinion.

There is a satisfying conclusion that restates the opinion.

Support for opinion includes convincing facts, explanations, examples, statistics, expert quotes, and description.

Organization includes coherent paragraphs with transition words and phrases.

The writing is about one topic.

There is variety in sentence structure and word choice.

The writing sounds honest and sincere.

Comments—strengths and/or weaknesses (grades 3–6 students write comments on sticky notes for immediate application).

Appendix 5 **Conference Notes for Argumentative Writing**

Name_____ **Date** _____

Introduction provides a claim that has pros and cons.

There is a satisfying conclusion that restates the claim with a strong statement.

Organization includes convincing facts supported with examples, explanations, statistics, and expert quotes.

The writing is about one topic but presents both sides, refuting one of them logically.

There is variety in sentence structure and word choice.

The writing sounds like it addresses a target audience.

Comments—strengths and/or weaknesses (grades 5–8 students write comments on sticky notes for immediate application).

Appendix 6 **Notice, Ponder, Polish Conference**

Name _____ **Date** _____

Title of Piece: _____

_____

_____

Noticings: _____

_____

_____

Questions: _____

_____

_____

Polishes: _____

_____

_____

Mini-Lesson Possibilities: _____

_____

_____

_____

Appendix 7 Ways to Respond

POINTING

I LIKE THE PART WHEN YOU SAID . . .

I LIKED THE WORDS . . .

. . . STUCK IN MY MIND AFTER YOU FINISHED YOUR READING.

I WANTED TO KNOW MORE ABOUT . . .

SUMMARIZING

I THINK THE MAIN POINT WAS . . .

TO ME YOUR STORY SAYS . . .

TO ME THE WORD . . . SUMMARIZES YOUR WRITING.

TELLING

WHEN YOU SAID . . . IT MADE ME THINK OF . . .

I FELT . . . WHEN YOU READ YOUR STORY.

I WONDERED . . . WHEN YOU SAID . . .

Appendix 8   Notice, Ponder, Polish Form

NPP Response from _____

To _____ **Date** _____

Title of Piece _____

Notice:

Ponder:

Polish:

- -

NPP Response from _____

To _____ **Date** _____

Title of Piece _____

Notice:

Ponder:

Polish:

Appendix 9 NPP Sentence Stems (Notice, Ponder, Polish)

Notice:

1. I like the part where _____ .

2. Your efforts helped me feel _____ .

3. You can feel proud of _____ .

4. Hats off to you because _____ .

Ponder:

1. I wonder _____ .

2. Tell me more about _____ .

3. Did you mean _____ ?

4. I was a little confused about _____ .

Polish:

1. Maybe you could _____ .

2. Had you thought of _____ ?

3. Here's an idea _____ .

4. Once I _____ .

Appendix 10 **Peer Conference Reports**

Peer Conference Report

Writer _____ **Date** _____

Writing Partner _____

My partner noticed _____

_____

My partner asked _____

_____

One revision might be _____

_____

- -

Peer Conference Report

Writer _____ **Date** _____

Writing Partner _____

My partner noticed _____

_____

My partner asked _____

_____

One revision might be _____

_____

Appendix 11 **Peer Conference Response Form**

Author

Author's Name _____

Conference Partner _____ Date _____

Mentor Text (if applicable) _____

_____

- -

Partner

I like _____

_____

_____

The questions I have are:

1. _____

2. _____

3. _____

One thing you might think about doing is _____

_____

- -

Author

What did you change? _____

_____

Why? _____

_____

A Closer Look: Learning More About Our Writers with Formative Assessment, K–6 by Lynne R. Dorfman and Diane Dougherty. © 2017. Stenhouse Publishers.

Appendix 12 Peer Response Share (Grades K–2)

Author's Name _____

Title _____

Partner's Name _____

Circle one.

I like your . . .

     title   story   character(s)

This is why: _____

_____

_____

Circle one.

Maybe you can add . . .

     color words   a setting   a different title

     a character's feelings   the characters' names   an ending

REFERENCES

Ackerman, Kristin, and Jennifer McDonough. 2016. *Conferring with Young Writers: What to Do When You Don't Know What to Do*. Portland, ME: Stenhouse.

Anderson, Carl. 2000. *How's It Going? A Practical Guide to Conferring with Student Writers*. Portsmouth, NH: Heinemann.

———. 2005. *Assessing Writers*. Portsmouth, NH: Heinemann.

Atwell, Nancie.1987. *In the Middle: Writing, Reading, and Learning with Adolescents*. Portsmouth, NH: Heinemann.

———. 1998. *In the Middle: New Understandings About Writing, Reading, and Learning*. 2nd ed. Portsmouth, NH: Heinemann.

Averbeck, Jim. 2015. *One Word from Sophia*. New York: Atheneum Books for Young Readers.

Ayres, Ruth, and Stacey Shubitz. 2010. *Day by Day: Refining Writing Workshop Through 180 Days of Reflective Practice*. Portland, ME: Stenhouse.

Beasley, Cassie. 2015. *Circus Mirandus*. New York: Penguin.

Berger, Ron, Leah Rugen, and Libby Woodfin. 2013. *Leaders of Their Own Learning: Transforming Schools Through Student-Engaged Assessment*. Hoboken, NJ: Wiley.

Berne, Jennifer. 2013. *On a Beam of Light: A Story of Albert Einstein*. San Francisco: Chronicle Books.

Berne, Jennifer, and Sophie Degener. 2015. *The One-on-One Reading & Writing Conference: Working with Students on Complex Texts*. New York: Teachers College Press.

Boelts, Maribeth. 2014. *Happy Like Soccer*. Somerville, MA: Candlewick Press.

Brookhart, Susan M. 2013. *How to Create and Use Rubrics for Formative Assessment and Grading*. Alexandria, VA: ASCD.

Burgess, Matthew. 2015. *Enormous Smallness: The Sweet Illustrated Story of E. E. Cummings and His Creative Bravery*. New York: Enchanted Lion Books.

Burleigh, Robert. 2003. *Home Run: The Story of Babe Ruth*. New York: Houghton Mifflin.

Cain, Janan. 2000. *The Way I Feel*. Seattle, WA: Parenting Press.

Calkins, Lucy, and Mary Ehrenworth. 2016. "Growing Extraordinary Writers: Leadership Decisions to Raise the Level of Writing Across a School and a District." *Reading Teacher* 70 (10): 7–18.

Common Core State Standards Initiative. 2014. *English Language Arts Standards*. www.corestandards.org/ELA-Literacy/.

Cook, Julia. 2006. *My Mouth Is a Volcano!* Chattanooga, TN: National Center for Youth Issues.

Creech, Sharon. 2001. *A Fine, Fine School*. New York: HarperCollins.

Crews, Donald. 1998. *Night at the Fair*. New York: Greenwillow Books.

Davies, Nicola. 2005. *One Tiny Turtle*. New York: Penguin Random House.

Davis, Kathryn Gibbs. 2014. *Mr. Ferris and His Wheel*. New York: Houghton Mifflin Harcourt Books for Young Readers.

Dorfman, Lynne, and Diane Dougherty. 2014. *Grammar Matters: Lessons, Tips, and Conversations Using Mentor Texts, K–6*. Portland, ME: Stenhouse.

Duckor, Brent. 2014. "Formative Assessment in Seven Good Moves." *Educational Leadership* 70 (6): 28–32.

Dweck, Carol S. 2006. *Mindset: The New Psychology of Success; How We Can Learn to Fulfill Our Potential*. New York: Ballantine Books.

Fleming, Candace. 2002. *Muncha! Muncha! Muncha!* New York: Atheneum Books.

Fletcher, Ralph, and Joann Portalupi. 2001. *Writing Workshop: The Essential Guide*. Portsmouth, NH: Heinemann.

Fox, Mem. 1992. *Night Noises*. Boston: Houghton Mifflin Harcourt Books for Young Readers.

The Glossary of Educational Reform. www.edglossary.org/assessment.

Glover, Matt. 2014. "Vision and Choice in the K–3 Writing Workshop." In *Write Now! Empowering Writers in Today's K–6 Classrooms*, ed. Kathy Ganske. Newark, DE: International Reading Association.

Hattie, John. 2012. *Visible Learning for Teachers: Maximizing Impact on Learning*. New York: Routledge.

Hewitt, Geof. 1995. *A Portfolio Primer: Teaching, Collecting, and Assessing Student Writing*. Portsmouth, NH: Heinemann.

Hopkinson, Deborah. 2012. *Sky Boys: How They Built the Empire State Building*. New York: Schwartz and Wade.

Idle, Molly. 2014. *Flora and the Penguin*. San Francisco: Chronicle Books.

Johnston, Peter. 2004. *Choice Words: How Our Language Affects Children's Learning*. Portland, ME: Stenhouse.

———. 2012. *Opening Minds: Using Language to Change Lives*. Portland, ME: Stenhouse.

Johnston, Tony. 1990. *Amber on the Mountain*. New York: Puffin Books.

Kear, Dennis J., Gerry A. Coffman, Michael C. McKenna, and Anthony Ambrosio. 2000. "Measuring Attitude Toward Writing: A New Tool for Teachers." *Reading Teacher* 54 (1): 10–23.

Kearney, Meg. 2013. *Trouper*. New York: Scholastic Press.

Landrigan, Clare, and Tammy Mulligan. 2013. *Assessment in Perspective: Focusing on the Reader Behind the Numbers*. Portland, ME: Stenhouse.

Leahy, Siobhan, Christine Lyon, Marnie Thompson, and Dylan Wiliam. 2005. "Classroom Assessment: Minute by Minute, Day by Day." *Educational Leadership* 63 (3): 19–24.

Miller, Debbie. 2013. *Reading with Meaning: Teaching Comprehension in the Primary Grades*. Portland, ME: Stenhouse.

Mraz, Kristine, and Christine Hertz. 2015. *A Mindset for Learning: Teaching the Traits of Joyful, Independent Growth*. Portsmouth, NH: Heinemann.

Murawski, Darlyne A. 2000. *Bug Faces*. Washington, D.C.: National Geographic Children's Books.

Murphy, Frank. 2015. *Take a Hike, Teddy Roosevelt!* New York: Random House Children's Books.

Murray, Donald M. 1982. *Learning by Teaching*. Portsmouth, NH: Heinemann.

———. 1985. *A Writer Teaches Writing*. 2nd ed. Boston: Houghton Mifflin.

NCTE Position Statement: A statement on an educational issue approved by the NCTE Board of Directors or the NCTE Executive Committee. 2013. "Formative Assessment That *Truly* Informs Instruction," October 21.

Overmeyer, Mark. 2005. *When Writing Workshop Isn't Working: Answers to Ten Tough Questions, Grades 2–5*. Portland: ME: Stenhouse.

———. 2009. *What Student Writing Teaches Us: Formative Assessment in the Writing Workshop*. Portland, ME: Stenhouse.

———. 2015. *Let's Talk: One-on-One, Peer, and Small-Group Conferences*. Portland, ME: Stenhouse.

Owocki, Gretchen, and Yetta Goodman. 2002. *Kidwatching: Documenting Children's Literacy Development*. Portsmouth, NH: Heinemann.

Palatini, Margie. 2003. *The Perfect Pet*. New York: HarperCollins.

Quate, Stevi, and John McDermott. 2014. "The Just-Right Challenge." *Educational Leadership* 72 (1): 61–65.

Ray, Katie Wood, and Lester L. Laminack. 2001. *The Writing Workshop: Working Through the Hard Parts (And They're All Hard Parts)*. Urbana, IL: NCTE.

Routman, Regie. 2000. *Conversations: Strategies for Teaching, Learning, and Evaluating*. Portsmouth, NH: Heinemann.

———. 2005. *Writing Essentials: Raising Expectations and Results While Simplifying Teaching*. Portsmouth, NH: Heinemann.

Rylant, Cynthia. 2015. *In November*. Boston: Houghton Mifflin Harcourt Books for Young Readers.

Sackstein, Starr. 2015a. *Hacking Assessment: 10 Ways to Go Gradeless in a Traditional Grades School*. Cleveland, OH: Times 10 Publications.

————. 2015b. *Teaching Students to Self-Assess: How Do I Help Students Reflect and Grow as Learners?* Alexandria, VA: ASCD.

Schertle, Alice. 1995. *Down the Road.* New York: Harcourt Children's Books.

Smith, Frank. 1988. *Joining the Literacy Club: Further Essays into Education.* Portsmouth, NH: Heinemann.

Spandel, Vicki. 2005. *The 9 Rights of Every Writer: A Guide for Teachers.* Portsmouth, NH: Heinemann.

————. 2012. *Creating Writers: 6 Traits Process, Workshop, and Literature.* 6th ed. New York: Pearson.

Stinson, Kathy. 1960. *Red Is Best.* New York: Open Road Media.

Swallow, Pamela. 2005. *Groundhog Gets a Say.* New York: Putnam.

Tomlinson, Carol Ann, and Tonya R. Moon. 2013. *Assessment and Student Success in a Differentiated Classroom.* Alexandria, VA: ASCD.

Tovani, Cris. 2011. *So What Do They Really Know? Assessment That Informs Teaching and Learning.* Portland, ME: Stenhouse.

Upjohn, Rebecca. 2007. *Lily and the Paper Man.* Toronto, ON: Second Story Press.

Viorst, Judith. 1987. *Alexander and the Terrible, Horrible, No Good, Very Bad Day.* New York: Atheneum Books for Young Readers.

Vygotsky, Lev S. 1989. *Thought and Language.* Cambridge, MA: MIT Press.

Wiggins, Grant. 2012. "Seven Keys to Effective Feedback." *Educational Leadership* 70 (1): 10–16.

Willems, Mo. 2003. *Don't Let the Pigeon Drive the Bus!* New York: Hyperion Books.

————. 2014. *The Pigeon Needs a Bath!* New York: Disney-Hyperion.

Yamada, Kobi. 2013. *What Do You Do with an Idea?* Seattle, WA: Compendium.

Zimbler, Suzanne. 2016. "Wild, Wild, Pets." *Time for Kids* 11 (6): 4–5.

INDEX